THE NEW RAILWAY

The Earliest Years of the West Highland Line

THE NEW RAILWAY

The Earliest Years of the West Highland Line

JOHN MCGREGOR

AMBERLEY

In memory of David Whitehead

Front cover, top: North British Railway: 'West Highland Bogie' 4-4-0 at Fort William. (J. L. Stevenson collection)
Front cover, bottom: West Highland Railway under construction – Loch Treig. (J. L. Stevenson collection)
Back cover: West Highland train at Bridge of Orchy, *c.* 1914. (J. Alsop collection)

First published 2015

Amberley Publishing
The Hill, Stroud
Gloucestershire, GL5 4EP

www.amberley-books.com

British Library Cataloguing in Publication Data.
A catalogue record for this book is available from the British Library.

ISBN 978 1 4456 4732 6 (print)
ISBN 978 1 4456 4733 3 (ebook)

Typeset in 10pt on 13pt Sabon.
Typesetting and Origination by Amberley Publishing.
Printed in the UK.

Contents

Acknowledgements

The railway politics of the Scottish Highlands are here combined with snatches of social history. I'm grateful to Georgina Coleby of Amberley Publishing, who recognised that this mixture had possibilities, and to her colleagues Louis Archard and Claire Hopkins, who helped refine it.

Opposite: Fort William and Ben Nevis in 1894. *(Mountain, Moor and Loch)*

Introduction

Together, the West Highland Railway proper and the West Highland Mallaig Extension form a 140-mile route (with reversal at Fort William). However, Roshven on Loch Ailort had been the west-coast harbour first intended – which Parliament rejected. Construction to Fort William began in 1889, but with no certainty of continuation to the western seaboard. Connecting with the Caledonian Canal, the 1½-mile Banavie branch would remain for half a dozen years the West Highland's extremity. At Crianlarich, the West Highland intersected the older Callander & Oban Railway; among the prospective benefits were shorter journeys between Glasgow and Oban, a rail connection from Lochaber eastwards to Stirling and additional 'circulars' for summer tourists. But the Crianlarich spur, lying unused into 1897, would carry little exchange traffic thereafter.

The West Highland might be extended, sooner or later, through the Great Glen to Inverness, breaching the Highland Railway's monopoly of the North. The promoters denied such intentions, in the short run at least, while asserting that connection at Inverness (like connection at Crianlarich) would be to the long-term advantage of the already-established companies. They submitted to a formal treaty, keeping the Great Glen rail-less in the short run – the so-called Ten Years Truce. Battle had been postponed, but not averted. Undermined in 1893, the Great Glen Agreement would collapse in 1894. Repaired, it would crumble again when the Invergarry & Fort Augustus Railway obtained Parliamentary approval in 1896.

The line to Mallaig, opened in 1901, endures. Thanks to the Crianlarich spur, the western half of the Oban line has survived since 1966 as a West Highland appendage (but the Callander & Oban, senior to the upstart West Highland, lives on in local memory). The Invergarry & Fort Augustus and its might-have-been Inverness extension have become history. This book addresses the West Highland's earliest years: when winning through to Mallaig and advance to Inverness alike were uncertain; when interchange at Crianlarich might yet have become meaningful; when a cross-country link into Strathspey and branches to Ballachulish and to Inveraray were projects still entertained. Traffic to Fort William (1894) and Banavie (1895) commenced amid mingled expectations and doubts. Railway politics inevitably enter – the North British Company, in agreeing to guarantee, work and maintain the West Highland, had incurred the enmity of the Caledonian (working the Callander & Oban) and made the Highland fearful for the future. But there is another side – dramas and disappointments, personalities and practicalities. 100 miles in length, tenuous and exacting, the new railway was unlike any other constituent of the North British system.

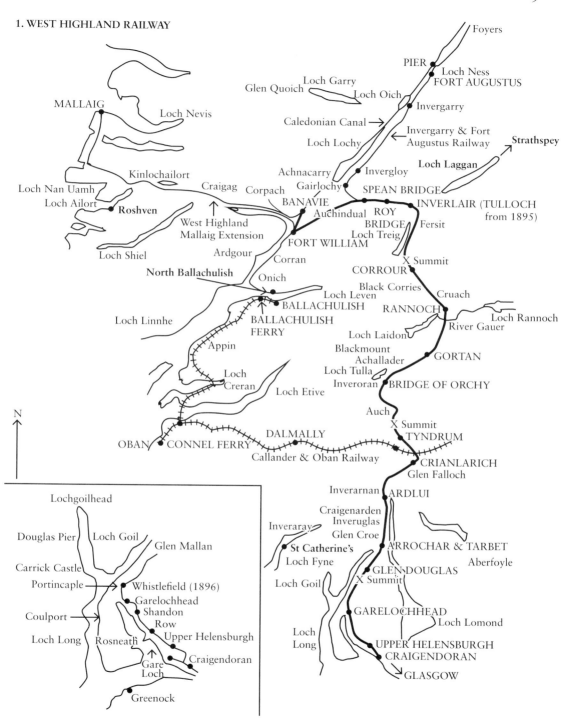

1. WEST HIGHLAND RAILWAY

Note: Lochaber is centred on Fort William, with Brae Lochaber (broadly Glen Spean and Glen Roy) to the north and Nether Lochaber to the south.

Chapter 1

Background

What impelled the North British to go adventuring in the western Highlands? There is no one answer.

The Highland Railway was formed by amalgamation in 1865 when the associated Inverness companies had already reached east to Elgin and Keith, south to Perth and north to Bonar Bridge. Ten years later the Highland system would extend to Strome Ferry, the then terminus of the Dingwall & Skye Railway, and to Wick and Thurso, thus completing the Far North line. It was a striking achievement; but the Highland's solvency depended on concentrating all possible through traffic on their Perth–Inverness main line, the acknowledged rail artery of the North. Other definitive amalgamations marked the 1860s. The North British Company joined first with the Edinburgh, Perth & Dundee, and then with the Edinburgh & Glasgow. The Caledonian, their great rival, acquired the Scottish Central and then the Scottish North Eastern. Though the two enemies remained roughly equal by route miles, the enlarged Caledonian emerged more coherent, more strongly placed. Both exchanged traffic with the Highland Railway, but the larger share fell to the Caledonian Company, who remitted payment for Highland entry to Perth over their track (from Stanley Junction) in return for favourable treatment. In vain, the North British urged that the Highland end a servile relationship. ('I cannot understand,' wrote John Walker, the North British general manager, to Andrew Dougall, who commanded at Inverness, 'why a large and fairly prosperous company like yours should, for the sake of £5,000 a year, sacrifice its independence.') Meanwhile, the Callander & Oban Railway, authorised in 1865 with Scottish Central backing, had become a Caledonian client and dealt sparingly with the North British. After stop-go progress westward, the line finally opened to Oban in 1880.

The North British had some advantages: the enlarged company was strongly posted across the Central Belt, with railheads at the edge of the Highlands – Helensburgh (on the Clyde estuary), Balloch (Loch Lomond) and, from 1883, Aberfoyle (in the Trossachs). Approached by hopeful protagonists of a 'direct' westerly rail route to the North, the directors thought wistfully of independent access to Inverness. A line of this stamp would both provide a cut-off to Oban and improve by 40 miles the established Stirling–Perth–Inverness route, which detoured by Forres; it would breach the Highland Company's monopoly and capture Inverness traffic from the Caledonian. But the North British were irresolute, their resources otherwise engaged. (Dominance of Fife and the Borders had been haphazardly and expensively achieved.) Not until the mid-1880s, with conquest of the Forth and Tay water breaks at last in sight, could they look seriously beyond the unification of their bits-and-pieces system to more determined expansion.

And by then there were other imperatives. The Scottish Highlands began to attract speculative railway ventures, for which opportunities elsewhere in Britain had diminished. Caledonian and North British, and the Highland Company too, would have to reckon with unpredictable outside promotions ('contractors' lines'), and the outsiders behind them could not be controlled. Moreover, government attention had been drawn to the Highlands and Islands. Agitation, prompted by injustice and poverty, turned to disorder in the so-called Crofters' War. The ensuing Napier Commission (1883–4) would recommend, albeit tentatively, transport improvements subsidised by the taxpayer. Here was both incentive and respectable cover for speculative schemes.

Contractors, engineers and would-be promoters had seen possibilities in the chequered fortunes of the Callander & Oban Railway, halted at Tyndrum from 1873 to 1877. Narrow-gauge feeder lines were proposed, both from Oban and from Fort William. Earlier plans for a direct Glasgow–Oban line via Loch Lomond were revived in the hope of North British patronage, and this in turn influenced the Caledonian decision to see their protégé finished to Oban. With the Callander & Oban open throughout, speculative interest did not abate; it fastened instead on a possible cut-off to Crianlarich, shortening the Glasgow–Oban journey. The North British were again tempted – but what if the Caledonian found attack the best means of defence? A Glasgow–Crianlarich cut-off endorsed by the Caledonian would not only safeguard their Oban traffic, it would facilitate Caledonian penetration of North British territory. Walker of the North British coveted running powers to Oban. When he spoke of 'going to Crianlarich', however, he had in mind pre-emptive action to protect his company's Dunbartonshire and Loch Lomond preserves.

Suddenly announced, the hugely ambitious Glasgow & North Western Railway (1882) was blatantly speculative. The 160-mile line would have run by Loch Lomond's eastern shore, Glen Coe and the Great Glen to Inverness, making junction with the Callander & Oban at Tyndrum. The promoters aimed to set Caledonian against North British, and both these companies against the Highland, calculating that, in the ensuing scramble, at least part of their scheme would be adopted. Testing the public mood, they promised an early branch from Fort William westward to the Arisaig coast, ostensibly to relieve under-employment and distress. All the evidence indicates an outside venture, not a North British project in disguise. The North British *were* drawn in, but hesitated between backing the Glasgow & North Western and merely threatening to do so, as a lever to extract better terms at Perth. Meanwhile,

Charles Forman. (Courtesy of the late Rev. Diana Forman)

Caledonian and Highland made common cause to defeat the scheme in Parliament (1883). The excitement was short-lived, but it influenced the Napier Commissioners, who specifically suggested state assistance for any railway which private enterprise brought to Fort William, in order that the line be continued to the western sea.

The legacy of the Glasgow & North Western was all-round suspicion, and a North British resolve to shape events. Authorised in 1887, the Clyde, Ardrishaig & Crinan Railway obtained a North British guarantee and working agreement. In Charles Forman of Formans & McCall, the landed promoters found a persuasive engineer who promised economy in construction. The scheme had severe limitations, relying as it did on two ferry connections – across the Firth of Clyde (Craigendoran-Hunter's Quay) and across Loch Fyne. However, the North British argued (to good effect) that Parliament should allow them to develop South Argyll, where Crinan could be made 'another Oban', with North Argyll left to the Callander & Oban Company, thus balancing North British and Caledonian interests. In 1887/8 came the Glen Falloch Railway. Though ostensibly a harmless 9-mile branch linking the Callander & Oban with Loch Lomond, it was in effect a locally promoted 'contractors' line', exploiting Caledonian–North British tensions. In Caledonian hands it would bar their rival from Crianlarich, but it also offered the North British a spearhead – the shaft (from Aberfoyle, from Balloch or from Helensburgh) might be added later. Alerted to this danger, the Caledonian contrived to have the Glen Falloch Bill withdrawn.

In 1889, the North British came forward to support the West Highland Railway, a better proposition than the Clyde, Ardrishaig & Crinan. (The latter, denied further help, would remain unbuilt: the company was wound up in 1892.) The West Highland promotion took shape over many months. With state assistance in prospect, would the Caledonian entertain a Callander & Oban branch to Ballachulish and Fort William, either from Tyndrum via Glen Coe or from Connel Ferry? Or could the North British be induced to look beyond Crianlarich? In any case the line should continue to the Arisaig seaboard, under whatever conditions government might prescribe. The Lochaber landowners looked first to the Callander & Oban, i.e. to the Caledonian Company, who were agreeable in principle (given adequate local subscription) though in no hurry to see the line built. Fort William preferred to cultivate the North British, hoping to 'keep clear of Oban'. A link with Connel via the Loch Linnhe coast might spell permanent subordination to the Argyll town, which had gained at Fort William's expense once rail-connected. [1] Besides it meant a very roundabout journey to Glasgow. The Callander & Oban Company, for their part, preferred the relatively populous Benderloch and Appin route to a line through empty Glen Coe.

The West Highland promoters eventually forged an understanding between 'country' (landowners, sporting tenants and factors) and the activists of Fort William. Cameron of Lochiel and Lord Abinger set out to contrive a proprietors' alliance all along the proposed route. The Colquhouns of Luss (Luss Trustees) were recruited, by adapting the scheme to their wishes. They already favoured an extension of the existing Glasgow-Helensburgh line (i.e. to Garelochhead or Arrochar). The Glasgow

Glen Falloch. *(Mountain, Moor and Loch)*

& North Western debacle, where powerful landlords had declared emphatically against an untrustworthy outside speculation, was not to be repeated. Superficially at least the West Highland was a native product, emulating the local endeavour and sacrifice that had sustained both the Callander & Oban and the constituent companies of the Highland Railway in their earliest years. This served partially to conceal North British involvement, and softened the speculative interest of engineer and contractor.

Charles Forman, who had already been commissioned by the Luss Trustees, extended his survey to Crianlarich, Fort William and the west coast. He costed a 130-mile line from Craigendoran (Helensburgh) to Roshven, running by Glen Coe. A more circuitous route across Rannoch Moor, entering Lochaber by Glen Spean, would be substituted before the West Highland Bill was lodged in November 1888. The prestigious contractor Lucas & Aird endorsed Forman's work and subsequently secured the West Highland contract. Abinger used his City contacts to assess how readily West Highland shares would be taken up, were the North British to endorse the scheme. He had the advice of contractor David Lucas. Edinburgh lawyers MacRae, Flett & Rennie, in association with MacKenzie & Smith of Fort William, sought out friendly witnesses and prepared the promoters' case. (Colin MacRae was a relative of the Colquhoun family. Fellow solicitor Nigel MacKenzie was provost of Fort William and factor for half-a-dozen proprietors in the western Highlands, including Lochiel.)

There was certainly subterfuge; the promoters, in their parliamentary evidence, were no more forthcoming than they could help. Both general manager Walker and North British secretary George Wieland had been in correspondence with Donald Boyd, a leading merchant of Fort William. Robert Yellowlees, previously a promoter of the unsuccessful Stirling & Western Direct Railway (1887/8) and well known to Walker, had introduced Forman to Boyd, MacKenzie and their associates.[2] Meeting Forman and MacRae at his Achnacarry seat, Lochiel had agreed that he and Abinger would canvas their fellow landowners, leaving engineer and lawyer to seek North British aid. ('The North British Company cannot make the railway without us, and we cannot make the railway without [them].') Lochiel guessed, as he later admitted, that the North British were already covertly engaged. (North British involvement had really begun in 1887-8, when Walker suggested a Helensburgh–Crianlarich line to the Luss Trustees, in conjunction with the then Glen Falloch scheme.) Lochiel stipulated that the proprietors' personal liabilities be capped at a figure reflecting the approximate cost of an unopposed bill. Opposition was certain, and the North British would shoulder the additional expense on the condition that the decision to fight a protracted parliamentary battle was theirs alone.

At the turn of 1888/9, Lochiel twice met with the North British directors and their chairman, the Marquess of Tweeddale, who were brought to offer a working and maintenance agreement, plus a guaranteed dividend (calculated on contributory traffic).[3] The North British later promised to find up to £150,000 of the initial capital. Walker

Statue of Donald Cameron of Lochiel, 24th chief of Clan Cameron, The Parade, Fort William. (Courtesy of A. Gillespie)

would declare that his company had taken no part before the West Highland promotion matured. Only then had the North British come forward to assist a worthy project, because the Caledonian Company had declined to do so. The Caledonian protested, unavailingly, at this mendacious account, and complained that the 'country' had deceived them by evincing continued enthusiasm for a branch from Connel Ferry and thus keeping the Callander & Oban in play until the West Highland Bill was prepared. They blamed in particular George Malcolm, factor for Glen Garry and Glen Quoich.

In an attempt to block the West Highland, the Caledonian hastily revived the Glen Falloch scheme of 1887/8 as a Callander & Oban bill. They promised to expedite a Connel Ferry–Ballachulish–Fort William line, provided the West Highland Bill was withdrawn. Oban, alleged the Caledonian, was the real target; the North British hoped to smuggle in running powers over the Callander & Oban west from Crianlarich: if these were granted, the route onwards to Lochaber would be abandoned. In the event, Parliament required that the West Highland be completed to Fort William as a single operation. The North British, whatever their first intentions, chose not to press for running powers, settling instead for exchange at Crianlarich. Inverness was not immediately threatened, and the Highland Company, unable this time to plead mortal injury, judged the battle lost when the House of Lords Committee pronounced favourably.[4] They ceased their opposition in the Commons on the condition that the West Highland did not advance into the Great Glen for a full ten years after traffic to Fort William had begun.

The Lords qualified their approval by striking out the West Highland's Roshven arm, which the North British excluded from their guarantee. Forman's survey west of Fort William had been less painstaking. The promoters wanted the shortest possible line to the coast – thus staking a claim for future subsidy. Roshven was expendable in the short term, though this strategy risked the whole project – because the creation of a new railhead for the western fishery, so much talked-up, would be postponed indefinitely. However, the Lords' decision eased negotiations with the Highland Company – with Roshven out of the reckoning, the Highland's traffic via Strome Ferry was for the moment safe. On North British advice, the proposed West Highland branch from Spean Bridge to the Caledonian Canal at Loch Lochy had been dropped already. A seeming probe towards Inverness, it might have driven the Highland Company to implacable resistance.

Caledonian and Highland had miscalculated, seeing Roshven as integral to the West Highland Bill, which, they hoped, would fail on the controversial question of government aid. Completion to Fort William was feasible under the North British guarantee, a matter only for the North British board and their shareholders. The guarantee also embraced the short branch to Banavie, at the southern end of the canal, to be included in the supplementary West Highland Bill of 1889/90, after the Great Glen Agreement was concluded. (The Highland thought the Banavie line harmless.) But could extension west from Banavie be achieved? And would the Great Glen treaty endure? For the West Highland Railway Bills/Acts of 1888–90 and the Great Glen Agreement of 1889, see Appendix.

Prospective Witnesses for 'Railway No.1' (Craigendoran - Crianlarich)

Captain Roderick Colquhoun "as to consent and interest of proprietors"

William Dunn, factor, Breadalbane estates "as to ditto and traffic on Northern portion of Railway".

James Wilson, factor, Luss Trustees estates "as to benefits to be derived by the country ... and as to traffic".

John Tawse, solicitor for Luss Trustees "as to ditto and specially as to his connection with former negotiations for construction of line"

Alexander Breingan, provost of Helensburgh "as to public feeling of that town and local advantages..".

James Morrison, Shandon Hydropathic Company "as to number of visitors to his establishment and benefits to the locality".

Alexander Logan, house agent, Glasgow and owner of house property, Garelochhead "as to benefits to that district and feeling of people, also as to tourist traffic."

A. Cameron, hotel keeper, Garelochhead "as to tourist traffic and visitors."

Parlan MacFarlane, tenant farmer "as to benefits to farms and population".

Duke of Argyll "as to benefits to Roseneath property and generally to the Highlands..".

Peter Stalker, hotel keeper, Arrochar "as to traffic of circular route from Loch Lomond to Loch Long".

William Menzies, tenant farmer "as to traffic in Glen Falloch".

Thomas MacLean, manager, North British Steam Packet Company "as to tourist traffic on board his steamers".

George MacLachlan, town clerk, Helensburgh "as to feelings ... in Helensburgh and district".

West Highland Railway Bill, 1888/9, prospective parliamentary witnesses. (Courtesy of the West Highland Museum, Fort William)

Chapter 2

Building

Scars of construction: West Highland Railway, looking north from Tarbet, Loch Lomond. (Author's collection)

In October 1889, Lucas & Aird broke ground at both ends of the authorised route (the 'first sod' ceremony was held at Lochy Bridge, outside Fort William) and at three intermediate locations. Of these five working bases, Helensburgh, Crianlarich and Tyndrum were served by existing railways, while Arrochar (Loch Long) and Fort William were supplied by the sea. (The contractor's traffic to Crianlarich and Tyndrum was some consolation for the Callander & Oban Company.) As building advanced, barges were employed on Loch Lomond between Tarbet and Ardlui, and a little steamer was placed on Loch Treig, where the line descended into Lochaber.

The terse West Highland Company minutes afford only glimpses of the construction years. For example, during 1890 the revised entry to Fort William entailed negotiations with the Belford Hospital Trustees, while in 1892 flooding in Glen Spean disrupted the contractor's programme. Lucas & Aird encountered more 'mixed excavation' than estimated and sought revised terms.[1] Deadlock ensued, amid a legal wrangle, during 1890/1. A resolution was found and Lucas & Aird resumed work, mollified by the early purchase of their West Highland shares, which the North British were pledged to buy on *completion* of the line. At the outset, 64,000 Scots fir sleepers were delivered to Fort William. Two years later, the directors approved a top-up order for rails (1,100 tons), chairs (750 tons), spikes (60 tons), fish-plates (33 tons) and bolts and nuts (12 tons), besides 12,000 additional sleepers. Formans & McCall provided biannual reports: by February 1892, the earthworks were 72 per cent complete south of Crianlarich, 63 per cent complete further north and 44 miles of permanent way had been laid; by September of that year, earthworks end-to-end were 83 per cent complete, with 70

Horseshoe Bend, Auch: West Highland Railway. (J. L. Stevenson collection)

Above: West Highland Railway – remains of a temporary (construction) siding at northern Horseshoe viaduct, Auch Glen. (Courtesy of Ewan Crawford)

Left: 'Renton boulder', Rannoch station, West Highland Railway. (Courtesy of J. Gray)

miles of permanent way in place; fencing was 60 per cent complete, and 68 miles of telegraph wire had been installed.

Our picture is enlarged by the North British Company's records. In August 1892 John Conacher, who succeeded John Walker (d. 1891) as general manager, came to see the works for himself. He was conducted over the line on either side of Crianlarich by Charles Forman, utilising Lucas & Aird's pug-engines. Thirty of these little locomotives were employed on the West Highland contract, including the pugs initially shipped to Fort William. Arriving by the Callander & Oban, Conacher was taken north beyond County March summit to the Horseshoe bend at Auch, then south to Loch Lomond and Loch Long. The two-day expedition embraced eight viaducts in various stages of completion, which surely meant scrambling, though temporary trestles were in place. Ahead of the tour, Forman had suggested that his visitor 'bring a few friends' but not, by implication, Mrs Conacher. In Glen Mallan the formation was unfinished. The Helensburgh squad, building north, and the Arrochar squad, building south, were not yet joined. But twelve months later a tenuous track stretched 70 miles from Craigendoran, on the North British Glasgow–Helensburgh line, into the heart of Rannoch – by which time the Fort William team, isolated from all the rest, had built through Brae Lochaber to the highest reach of Rannoch Moor.

The West Highland Company, independent on paper but really 'the North British by another name', was chaired by Lord Abinger. He soon gave way to Tweeddale, chairman of the North British, while George Wieland, the North British secretary, doubled as secretary of the West Highland. On 15 September 1893, representatives of both boards met at Cruach for a 'last spike' celebration. Several had come north in

Arrochar & Tarbet station (island and subway; dwarf signal cabin), West Highland Railway. (J. L. Stevenson collection)

Roy Bridge station (side platform; supplementary down-side building), West Highland Railway. (J. Alsop collection)

contractor John Aird's saloon, a journey not without adventure (they were required to cross at least one viaduct on foot). The final hammer stroke was made by financier James Renton, a West Highland director by virtue of his bridging loan – the company would require retrospective enlargement of their capital powers. Renton's was scarcely a selfless action; nevertheless, it met the immediate shortfall and the navvies, grateful that their employment would not again be interrupted, sculpted the 'Renton boulder', which stands today at Rannoch station.

The line was single-track throughout. Sites had been chosen during 1892 for a dozen intermediate stations, all with passing loops – Upper Helensburgh [sic], Row [sic], Shandon, Garelochhead, Tarbet & Arrochar [sic], Ardlui, Crianlarich, Tyndrum, Bridge of Orchy, Inverlair (subsequently Tulloch), Roy Bridge and Spean Bridge. Additional to Glen Douglas siding (i.e. passing place), between Garelochhead and Arrochar & Tarbet, passing loops were needed at Gortan (Gorton) and Lebruaridh (subsequently Corrour), breaking the long sections Bridge of Orchy–Rannoch and Rannoch–Inverlair. As the autumn of 1893 turned into a wet and stormy winter, it became imperative that fill and ballast was run through to Rannoch Moor. Clinker, ash and other industrial wastes were delivered in vast quantities to Craigendoran. The weighty ballast trains, hauled (cautiously) by North British locomotives, would identify 'soft' places while consolidating the line. North British drivers and firemen would be able to learn the road.

Near Gortan the formation was sustained by brushwood rafts, pickled in the oily bogs. These 'floating' embankments were troublesome. The critical thing, however, was the completion of the major structures. Steel erection (by Alexander Findlay & Co.) was,

Glen Falloch Viaduct, W. H. Railway

Glen Falloch viaduct, West Highland Railway. (J. Alsop collection)

in late 1893, well advanced, but several viaducts (including the highest of all, across the Dubh Eas burn in Glen Falloch) were not ready for heavy engines. Just after New Year 1894, North British inspector Alexander Hogg accompanied Forman along the entire route. Bridge testing, he noted, had reached Glen Douglas, and along the Gare Loch the line was already thoroughly ballasted. From Loch Lomond through Crianlarich and Tyndrum to Glen Orchy much remained to be done. Across Rannoch Moor there was no remedy for lack of fill, and the granite cutting at Cruach, bypassed by temporary track, had not been fully excavated. Onwards to Fort William, the line was 'practically completed'. Lucas & Aird had exploited as much as possible the sand and gravel that outcropped amid the Rannoch bogs. Ballast sidings had been established at Fersit, near the foot of Loch Treig, and at Auchindaul, between Spean Bridge and Fort William.

Hogg saw only desultory work north of Crianlarich. Forman explained that until the spring, the men were concentrated on the less exposed sections to the south, which Lucas & Aird confirmed. To defy the winter storms was counterproductive; it 'penalised the works' and accrued more repairs than progress. But the North British, set on opening the West Highland that summer, were unconvinced. Need *everything* be delayed? If foundations were put in, the subcontractors could begin the station buildings all the sooner. Aird demurred, 'It is impossible … to do more … To specify [a completion] date would only be misleading you.' He requested the loan of old North British coaches, in which navvies might take shelter when wind and rain were intermittent. Conacher consented and six 'uncushioned Thirds' were deployed across Rannoch Moor. Similar vehicles, sent to Fort William, formed a works train during the final months of construction.

North British Railway: goods 0-6-0 at Fort William shed. (J. Alsop collection)

April brought better conditions and longer days when Forman's bridge-proving extended beyond Bridge of Orchy. For this purpose he borrowed three North British locomotives – a 'heavy tank' coupled between 'two of your heaviest goods class'. Rannoch Moor became accessible from the south and North British 0-6-0s were soon in evidence, heading ballast trains and returning the empty wagons to Craigendoran. From May Conacher authorised double-shifting; with relief drivers and firemen, deliveries could continue during all the daylight hours of summer. As the shuttle intensified, Lucas & Aird allocated a pilot pug to safety duties (its passage gave warning of a following ballast train), while 'speaking instruments' afforded protection against error or misunderstanding.[2] These precautions no doubt prevented accidents, but there was at least one serious derailment (near Craigenarden on Lochlomondside). Livestock were frequent casualties, and farmers along the line, though generally supporters of the West Highland, expressed anger. Conacher hopefully proposed a July opening day, and to this end the Board of Trade indicated their readiness to examine all the viaducts, lesser bridges and culverts so far tested by Formans & McCall.

Major Francis Marindin RE, of the Board of Trade's Railway Department inspectorate, approved over 300 structures; he reached beyond Achallader viaduct in Strathtulla. But the North British representatives in attendance were dismayed to find so much else 'backward', not least the unstable embankments approaching the Gauer and Rannoch viaducts. The latter, immediately north of Rannoch station and

Rannoch viaduct, West Highland Railway. (J. Alsop collection)

the longest on the line, spanned a peaty depression beneath Cruach hill. In a sharp exchange, Conacher reproached Forman:

> A great many arrangements have been made in dependence on your assurance that [all] would be ready.

The engineer retorted that he had given no absolute promise:

> I have always said … everything depended on the weather … It is impossible to forecast what contingencies may arise. For instance, in the past fortnight … the men lost four days …

Marindin's *general* inspection was imminent when Forman at last declared that a continuous permanent way was accomplished fact, but he added that the 'big banks' on Rannoch Moor still required 'a good deal of lifting' [sic].

Between Tuesday 3 July and Friday 6 July the inspection party, which included Forman and several North British departmental officers, moved systematically north. While Marindin judged the line well engineered, the catalogue of defects mounted. Forman, by one less-than-friendly account, blustered that all could be put right quickly, at which Marindin murmured in biblical tones, 'Blessed are they who expect nothing, for they shall not be disappointed!' The succession of unfinished stations all the way to Rannoch had already told against a favourable decision when disaster clinched the matter: a summer cloudburst, overwhelming a culvert, washed out the formation above Achallader. A ballast empties tumbled into the gap and the fireman was fatally injured. The inspector's train, returning to Tyndrum for the weekend, had passed the spot half an hour before, battered by (in Marindin's words) 'a most fearful thunderstorm'. That Saturday Marindin viewed the hastily restored embankment. On Monday 9 July he resumed his inspection, casting a dubious eye over the 'big banks' and unfinished Cruach cutting. He arrived in Fort William the same evening. Save for the half-built stations in Glen Spean (Inverlair, Roy Bridge and Spean Bridge), he found that the West Highland's final 30 miles were all but ready.[3] But a delicate problem awaited him (see Chapter 4). Time and again disappointed, Fort William had obtained the sure promise of rail connection, only to quarrel with the West Highland Company over occupation of the foreshore.

Of the principal individuals in this narrative a good deal is known: Cameron of Lochiel, whose advocacy (so he claimed) had swayed the North British directors to back the West Highland project; John Conacher, wary of his predecessor's commitments and impatient to have the West Highland open for traffic, when the line's earning capacity could be tested; John Aird, contractor, MP and art collector; Charles Forman, restless for new opportunities and, as the North British reckoned, too much his own man … There are other glimpses: of John Blue, Lucas & Aird's section engineer on Rannoch Moor, whose next posting, by contrast, was to Egypt's Aswan Dam on the Nile river; of 'amiable Mr Slocombe', whose sketches illustrated *Mountain, Moor and Loch*, the first official guide to the West Highland. Over several weeks Slocombe hitched rides on ballast trains, witnessed bridge testing and endured the rain, only complaining that his favourite London tobacco was unobtainable.

Of the navvies who built the West Highland we can know relatively little, though their alleged misdeeds are recorded – fouling of the River Falloch and River Orchy was the recurring complaint of sporting tenants on the Breadalbane estates. Lucas & Aird, good employers by the standards of the day, applied the lessons of their overseas contracts. Construction camps were spaced along the route, and to one exuberant journalist the orderly red-roofed huts beside Loch Long resembled 'a holiday village'. The typical hut had glazed windows, a stove, adequate ventilation, a separate room for the hut keeper and surface drains round the perimeter; in the dormitory sections were two tiers of beds. Dry earth closets stood apart. Many navvies and general labourers still chose to fend for themselves in lodgings (sparingly available along the southern half of the line), improvised huts or turf bothies. Explosions, rock falls and other hazards brought the usual quota of fatal accidents, but other deaths can be put down, in part at least, to makeshift dwellings. The winter of 1892/3 saw an outbreak of smallpox, and 'hot-bedding' may have contributed. The allocation, in the contractor's managed accommodation, was one bunk per two men, working shift-and-shift.

On the northern sections, with much of the line inaccessible, there was organised medical provision. Four-bed hospitals were established at Crianlarich and Rannoch, each with qualified assistants and two nurses, who offered maternity care to navvy wives and partners. Crianlarich had a dispensary and, briefly, a resident doctor. Gangers were instructed in first aid; they carried bandages and tourniquets, as did the pug drivers. Storemen stocked dressings and, for minor maladies, the 'ordinary remedies'. Via the 'speaking instruments' (above), professional advice could be obtained. Serious cases were brought as speedily as possible to Fort William. In several emergencies the steam lighter on Loch Treig proved a vital link. By 1893/4, when the line was more-or-less continuous, the medical assistants could make regular patrols.4

Marindin undertook to return three or four weeks later, hinting that he would be indulgent in everything inessential. The North British might count on an August opening. A price would be paid later for beginning traffic on these terms; but Conacher and his chairman insisted that the entire line be brought into use, before the summer season of 1894 ran out. Forman's suggestion of a preliminary opening, to Garelochhead, was rejected. Engine servicing was one essential. When Matthew Holmes, the North British locomotive superintendent, 'took a run to Fort William', he found only the turntable and water tank in place. His men must be able to draw their fires:

> We may do without a shed for a few weeks but we should have a pit at least sixty feet in length in the siding where the shed is to be erected.

Interlocked points and signals were absolutely necessary. Saxby & Farmer were yet to test sighting distances, erect posts and adjust semaphores and signal lamps. Tablet (token) equipment for single-line operation had to be made secure, despite the unfinished state of the stations.

In the interval between inspections, *Mountain, Moor and Loch* was printed, replete with history in the genre of Scott and Stevenson. To placate disgruntled farmers, G. B. Smith & Co. revisited their work, straining all the fences, while Lucas & Aird promised to level, on request, any hillocks outside railway ground from which sheep could jump. David Deuchars, North British superintendent of the line (i.e. head of traffic) and Conacher's deputy, had prepared a provisional passenger timetable, which was now modified in the expectation that Marindin would impose stringent speed restrictions. And an urgent search began for a guest of honour (royal if possible!) to grace the delayed opening day. This duty fell, in the end, to Lady Tweeddale. (Though not royal, the Marchioness was at least a lady of fashion, who had featured in Society magazines.)

On Saturday 28 July, Aird went carefully over the entire line. Telegrams to an anxious Conacher, waiting in Edinburgh, punctuated his journey. From Fort William, the ultimate message read:

> Great progress has been made and efforts continue. Have wired Marindin and see him Tuesday morning in London.

For a new railway, the track was now everywhere in good order, though ballasting was on-going. (500 wagons of ash would be delivered in the following week.) No

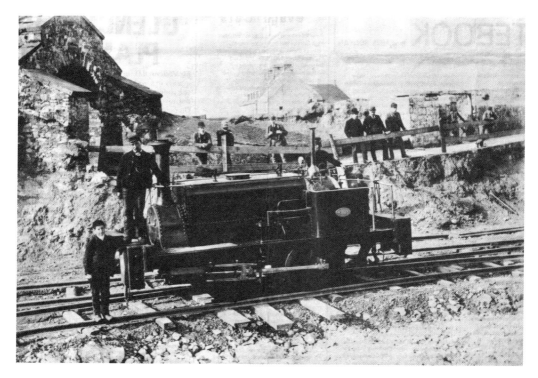

Lucas & Aird 'pug' at old fort, Fort William. (Courtesy of the West Highland Museum, Fort William)

station building was entirely ready, but Aird trusted to the inspector's good will. The agents (stationmasters) newly appointed to the West Highland, he advised, should be at their posts in good time, tidying up as best they could. Sufficiently reassured by Aird's report, Marindin made a brisk re-inspection, beginning at Craigendoran, on Thursday-into-Friday, 2/3 August. This time Deuchars accompanied him, and the North British had their desire: the Board of Trade would pass the line. Moreover, the inspector partially relented in respect of speed; having intended an *absolute* 25 mph limit, he conceded a 25 mph *average*. (Instead of going directly south, Marindin was diverted to an accident at Newtonmore, on the Highland Railway, and left by the Fort William–Kingussie coach. He authorised Forman to conduct a timing run and made his decision after seeing the results. The engine driver was instructed to use his own judgement wherever no explicit restrictions applied.)

Nevertheless it was touch and go, as Deuchars's Friday evening telegram to Conacher indicates:

We require Monday for [taking possession], after all the contractor's engines have been withdrawn, [and] passenger carriages and other plant will be brought up during the day.

Old fort gate, re-erected – Craigs Cemetery, Fort William. (Author's collection)

Over Saturday and Sunday, points and signals were double-checked and adjusted to meet Marindin's final requirements. Sets of the new bogie coaches dedicated to the West Highland were run back and forth to ease their axle boxes after weeks of storage. A passenger service of three trains in each direction required that two sets be stabled at Fort William. Public traffic began on Tuesday 7 August and the official opening was confirmed for four days later.

Mrs Cameron-Campbell of Callart, feudal superior of Fort William, had made over the old fort to the West Highland Company. The outer walls, still with sally port and jutting into the tides, were untouched. On the landward side, a temporary platform for the opening ceremony had already been erected alongside the main line. Here Lucas & Aird, in levelling the defensive ditch and dog-leg entry, spared an ancient tree, which, according to local legend, had served as a gallows.[5] Of the two covered gates, one was rebuilt to dignify the town cemetery.

Chapter 3

Opening Day

In the anxious few weeks before the Board of Trade finally passed the West Highland Railway for traffic, many details demanded attention. Adhesive name labels were printed, to be attached to the station lamps. Platform weighing machines were ordered. The chalet-style intermediate stations, designed by James Miller, stood for the most part internally incomplete, but their alpine motif was evident. Conacher ordered that timetables and other necessary notices be sensitively displayed; the shingle-clad buildings must not be marred by brash commercial advertising. He also sought confirmation, on the impeccable authority of Bradshaw, that to open all at once 100 miles of railway through a thinly populated region, without branch or other connection, was without precedent in the United Kingdom.[1] That the North British had made this possible, at some cost to their shareholders, who could only wait hopefully for the West Highland to show a profit, would be the theme of Lord Tweeddale's opening day speech – in furthering government policy for the Highlands and Islands, his company had done their duty.

At Fort William, a battlemented arch 'decked out with heather and brackens and crowned with flags and medallions' was thrown over the main line; it surmounted a double gate 'made fast with a little gold padlock'. At midday on 11 August, men of the Cameron Highlanders Volunteers stood to attention on the temporary platform, and the Freemasons of Fort William lined the approaches, to await the official party who had left Glasgow 4 hours earlier. Their eleven-coach train was double-headed, the leading locomotive decorated with flags. The ceremony began at once. Presented with a miniature shield engraved 'WHR', to which a gold key was attached, the Marchioness of Tweeddale unlocked the gates, which were swung clear. Two pipers on the heather battlements struck up a lively tune and the train steamed slowly through the arch amid exploding fog signals and a cheering crowd. Her rewards were a superior copy of *Mountain, Moor and Loch* and an album of photographs illustrating the route. 'Beautifully bound in silver, with Celtic ornamentation,' the album displayed the Tweeddale arms, the North British arms and the West Highland seal.[2]

North British and West Highland directors headed the guest list.[3] Included in the travelling party were the principal North British departmental officers; the senior staff of

PROGRAMME.

A.M. 8.15.	Departure of special train with Guests from Queen Street (High Level), Station, Glasgow.
P.M. 12.45.	Opening Ceremony at the Old Fort, Fort William, by the Marchioness of Tweeddale.
1.15.	Lunch in Marquee, at Fort William, presided over by the Marquis of Tweeddale, Chairman of the West Highland Railway Company.
3.55.	Return of special train with Guests to Glasgow.
5.25.	Tea served in train at Rannoch Station.
8.20.	Special train due at Queen Street (High Level) Station, Glasgow.

West Highland Railway opening day programme, 11 August 1894. (Author's collection)

Formans & McCall; Lucus & Aird's own engineers; and Colin MacRae (of MacRae, Flett & Rennie – see Chapter 1), who had become the West Highland Company's solicitor. The elderly David MacBrayne, whose steamer services were woven into the economic and social life of the western Highlands and Islands, sent his two sons. Engineering and contracting were further represented by two eminent figures, Benjamin Hall Blyth and Sir William Arrol. The English companies partnering the North British had their envoys, as did the Glasgow & South Western Railway, accounted a North British ally. The Caledonian Company sent their deputy chairman, Sir James King. This was perhaps a conciliatory gesture: in 1889/90 King had been appointed to the Lothian Commission, who endorsed the West Highland Mallaig Extension (see Chapter 11). Edinburgh's Lord Provost, Sir James Russell, and Glasgow's Chief Constable, John Boyd, represented Scotland's two principal cities, now in railway communication with Lochaber. A guest out of the usual run was William Acworth, pioneer of popular railway literature, who enjoyed behind-the-scenes access to several companies, including the North British.

Among the dignitaries waiting at Fort William was solicitor (and banker and factor for good measure) Nigel MacKenzie. He could savour a personal triumph long in the making, clouded though it now was by the foreshore quarrel (see Chapter 4). In 1883, as proxy for Cameron of Lochiel (then a member of the Napier Commission) he had testified in support of the Glasgow & North Western Railway. In 1887/8, having instigated the press campaign from which the West Highland promotion evolved, he had brought town and landed interest to a common purpose. While MacRae sought out friendly testimony south of Crianlarich and co-ordinated the overall West Highland case, MacKenzie first precognosced all the prospective witnesses-in-favour from the districts onwards to Fort William and Roshven, and then refined their evidence for Parliament. In several instances he adjusted and advised a second time, after Roshven was lost in the House of Lords, to ensure the best possible showing in the Commons. A colourful figure, known everywhere by his initials – NB for Nigel Banks – MacKenzie was now the West Highland's local agent. In Lochaber's estimation the new railway was very much 'his'. (Using initials as nickname is a Scottish habit. The story still circulates, with versions in Gaelic, that two credulous old ladies of Fort William, encountering their first North British locomotive, noted with mingled pride and disapproval the lettering 'NBR' on the tender: it was, they agreed, MacKenzie's proper due but perhaps a little pretentious ...)

Of wider fame was Dr Alexander Stewart, a clergyman in the Episcopalian traditions of Appin, Ballachulish and Onich and an authority on Highland folklore and natural history. Dr Stewart, who wrote prolifically under the penname Nether Lochaber, had delighted the Caledonian by castigating the West Highland's amended, more roundabout route. Rannoch Moor was 'a wilderness of moss ... the dreariest in all the British Isles'; it could not, in fifty years, 'yield profit sufficient to ... grease the wagon wheels'. However, the rumoured West Highland extension south to Ballachulish had reconciled him to the North British, and he joined in the celebrations at Fort William. James Baillie of Dochfour made a dutiful appearance – a Great Glen landowner (at its northern end), he was Unionist Parliamentary candidate for Inverness-shire, but also a director of the Highland Company. Baillie was uncomfortably aware how railway development had divided opinion across the county, with those who looked to West Highland and North British ranged against Highland loyalists. The sitting Crofter-Liberal MP, Dr Donald MacGregor, did not attend.

Less than 4 hours were allowed before the special departed. All adjourned briskly to the adjacent marquee for an elaborate lunch and a formidable round of toasts and speeches. Food and drink, tables and chairs, waiters, potted plants (and the marquee itself) had been brought from Glasgow the previous day. The speakers were, for the most part, conventionally congratulatory and skirted the likelihood of new conflicts; but Tweeddale (who presided) and Lochiel both addressed the future more bluntly. The West Highland Mallaig Extension Act had just been accomplished (see Chapter 11). Would the Caledonian Company and the Highland cease their obstruction? Would the Liberal Government commit to state assistance for the Mallaig line, acknowledging what North British efforts had already achieved? Lochiel praised Dr MacGregor and other Crofter-Liberals, who had put pressure on the Treasury to decide speedily. But this tribute was more calculated than sincere. Lochiel and his fellow landlords detested 'these Radicals' who had swept most of the constituencies in the Highlands since the 1880s. No love was lost on either side.4

Hopes of a royal presence at Fort William had seemed, to the outside world, amusingly out of proportion. Railway openings were no longer great events. But Fort William of 1894 was determined to celebrate in the manner of the many towns that had welcomed *their* railways decades earlier. A general holiday was declared. The police commissioners (town council) formally paraded, with provost and bailies in full regalia.5 Banners decorated the high street. Flags flew from hotels and private houses. The Cameron Volunteers' pipe band marched and countermarched within the burgh bounds through all the long day. A 'well-known artiste in fireworks' had been engaged to provide an evening climax (in August, light lingered till 9 p.m.), when rockets shells and stars abounded: 'The public road … was … thronged with townspeople who gave vent to their appreciation in … ringing cheers as the final display, entitled "The Falls of Niagara", was concluded.'

Chapter 4

The Foreshore Quarrel

Fort William's seaward aspect was unattractive and in 1882/3, the Glasgow & North Western project had raised hopes of improvement. Though engineer Thomas Walrond-Smith chose a hillside alignment, the burgh commissioners invited him to follow the foreshore, siting his station at the pierhead.[1] Before second thoughts could arise or safeguards be agreed, the Glasgow & North Western was defeated. The lesson of Oban's experience – after an earlier scheme had threatened to blight Oban bay, the Callander & Oban were required to find a discreet entry via Glencruiten – seems to have gone unheeded. That Fort William might become the only intermediate centre on a new trunk line to Inverness was an entrancing prospect.

The promoters of the West Highland Railway intended to halt their main line at the old fort, adding a half-mile tramway to the town pier on Loch Linnhe (see Appendix). The burgh commissioners were confident that the ragged shoreline could be much enhanced. They envisaged a seawall and public esplanade (the latter to be maintained at the town's expense), with unobtrusive tracks. Steps and jetties (or boat slips) would be added, and the existing sewers would be extended well beyond low water. They wanted an 'inner' carriage drive and an 'outer' pedestrian way beside Loch Linnhe, with the tramway between. A draft protection clause was prepared for inclusion in the West Highland Bill of 1888/9:

> The Company … shall make the whole surface of the embankment of a uniform height … pave or otherwise form it … sink the rails … and … complete [it] with a substantial fence of an ornamental character … [The embankment] shall be available [to] the public … for the use of carts and other vehicles … to such extent as shall not interfere … with the full use of the rails …

A meeting with Charles Forman left the commissioners satisfied that the *spirit* of their formula would be respected. The promoters did not dissent, but neither did they agree. Later, MacRae, Flett & Rennie were soothingly, and perhaps deliberately, vague:

The Company will not overlook the interests of Fort William with which town their leading directors [i.e. Lord Abinger and Cameron of Lochiel] are so intimately associated.

The *letter* of the 1889 West Highland Act prescribed adequate access to the shore, with rights of way *across* (not *along*) the tramway to be determined by the Board of Trade. Disquiet first arose when, in November 1889, the West Highland Company lodged their supplementary bill (Act of 1890) (see Appendix). The Torlundy–Fort William deviation cut the grounds of Belford Hospital and invaded Craigs Cemetery. It was a warning that the West Highland and their North British overlord might behave highhandedly. Moreover, the tramway was to be extended across the pierhead to distiller MacDonald's quay (known as New Pier), which the West Highland had purchased. At a public meeting in January 1890, obstruction of the town pier was the first concern, but had the commissioners been altogether too trustful? Though all acknowledged their debt to ex-provost MacKenzie, who had contributed mightily to winning a railway, he was now in some degree compromised, as the West Highland's agent. It aroused comment that, as secretary for the Belford Hospital Trustees, he had just secured their consent to the deviation.

Between the piers, Fort William, *c.* 1965; station in the background. (J. L. Stevenson collection)

The commissioners did not oppose the 1889/90 Bill but sent the town clerk, solicitor Donald Fraser, to alert the Board of Trade. Fraser made a second London journey to seek clarification and to offer evidence if so required. Counsel for the West Highland reiterated that the company were bound by their 1889 Act, though without explaining how Fort William's protection clause would be interpreted. Forman was broadly reassuring. When the West Highland opened, most of MacDonald's traffic (barley, draff, whisky and coal) would be handled at the old fort goods yard. New Pier, though railway-owned, would be available to all-comers for 'merchandise trade', freeing the often congested town pier for passengers, light goods and parcels. The west-end beach, where fishing nets were dried, would be untouched.[2] At high tide the fishermen could discharge their catches at the sheltered basin between the piers, with the tramway conveniently alongside. Little wagon traffic would be worked up and down the seawall. The primary function of the tramway was, and had always been, a limited interchange of passengers and luggage between train and steamer.

Forman expected most travellers to find their own way between MacBrayne's vessels and the West Highland station, for which the obvious site was the fort. Only the vans of regular passenger services would be shunted up and down the tramway. Private saloons, horseboxes, carriage trucks and perhaps family saloons, which were still favoured by the well-to-do middle class, might be taken to and fro, especially in the tourist season, but not entire trains. On the levelled ground behind the seawall, the West Highland need reserve only a 15-foot width for track which would see intermittent use. The burgh could have the rest, to employ as the commissioners pleased. In all circumstances there would be sufficient room for a footpath paralleling the tramway. In addition, a passage through the seawall would preserve the little harbour towards the fort, used by local boat owners.[3]

Fort William's fears were for the moment relieved, and ownership of the entire foreshore was transferred from the Crown to the West Highland Company. But Forman had made a significant reservation: 'Station sites are not fixed at such an early stage.' Two years later the West Highland board would minute that passenger arrangements at Fort William were being reconsidered. In September 1893 came confirmation, surely a North British decision, that the main line would be taken down the seawall to a cramped three-platform station fronting the pierhead. An open promenade or carriage drive to relieve the High Street became impossible, though a seaside footway, paralleling the line, was still feasible. The North British refused to negotiate and in May 1894, the commissioners appealed to the Board of Trade.

The plaudits bestowed on MacKenzie turned to blame. He had previously warned, however, that the town's cherished plans were far from secure. Yet another local lawyer, Donald MacPhee, put the commissioners' case to the Railway Department prior to the penultimate examination of the West Highland in July. A *through* road along the seawall, inside the track, was the least that Fort William could accept, if indeed it was too late to remove the station to the old fort. The road must emerge at the pierhead, and to that end the West Highland should alter their seawall or purchase and partially demolish the Chevalier Hotel adjacent to the station. In discussions with Forman at Fort William, the commissioners made the same demands. He offered instead what he termed a 'new street', necessarily truncated by the station but well proportioned. For this purpose, the West Highland Company would release a 13-foot strip of land along their seawall line and contribute to the cost of acquiring decayed property in the town's existing Low Street.

With nothing resolved, Forman left to accompany Marindin on his end-to-end inspection. MacPhee, newly returned from London, was sent in pursuit, and on Friday 6 July he found engineer and inspector at Tyndrum, but to no avail – they were preoccupied by the washout and fatal accident in Strathtulla (see Chapter 2). On the evening of Monday 9th they reached Fort William where a telegram had arrived instructing Marindin that he must use his best endeavours to resolve the foreshore quarrel. James Bryce, President of the Board of Trade in the Liberal Government, had pledged to 'bring the parties together' after MP MacGregor tabled a parliamentary question. That very night 'at half-past ten o'clock', provost Young and town clerk Fraser, with MacPhee in support, presented themselves at the Alexandra Hotel to request that Forman meet with them at once. He declined.

On Tuesday 10th, Marindin examined the whole Fort William layout, including the old fort, seawall and station.[4] On Wednesday 11th the inspector presided when Forman sat down once more with the commissioners. MacPhee raised lesser complaints: the boat slips outside the seawall were incorrectly angled; the debris of construction still littered the shore. But the not-to-be esplanade was the heart of the matter. Forman refused to yield: the West Highland had 'no obligation whatsoever', and offering the footpath was an act of grace. By oversight, he admitted, detailed drawings of station and signal box had not been submitted to the Railway Department. Nevertheless, the West Highland had the right to erect 'whatever buildings might be required for railway purposes' on the ground which they had acquired. The North British officers who accompanied Marindin's inspection were gloomy. He was, they warned, likely to rule against the pierhead station, and in Edinburgh general manager Conacher prepared for an adverse verdict.

However, Marindin's full report (dated 16 July, in London) was judicious. The West Highland Company had built their seawall and modified the sewerage to the letter of their Acts. They were bound to implement whatever conditions the Board of Trade might make. He could not have approved, in any case, the commissioners' conception of a promenade shared by public and railway. A tramway, operated as the West Highland promoters had first proposed, ought to be enclosed. Had it been unfenced, he would have set conditions that precluded unrestricted driving or walking. However, Fort William deserved sympathy:

There was, beyond question, a Section proposed for insertion in the [1889] Act and agreed by the Company and the Commissioners … but this Section was not inserted …

Having hinted at sharp practice, Marindin gave the pierhead terminus his lukewarm approval:

> Although ... there is [nothing] to object to in the Station itself, the originally proposed site strikes me as the better one.

To offset the town's bad bargain, the inspector recommended a generous reading, in the commissioners' favour, of the narrow clause ensuring access to the shore over the railway, on which the West Highland relied. He stipulated a fenced-off seaward footpath from the level crossing, which accessed the engine shed and goods yard, to the station; a footbridge at the station throat and another at the signal box; and a pedestrian right of way through the station to the pierhead. Thus, the slips and steps might be reached from every direction. With local fishing in decline these provisions appear, in hindsight, over-elaborate and no substitute for a lost esplanade. However, the commissioners' dignity was in some measure assuaged.

The West Highland was now all but certain to open within a few weeks, and a tacit truce emerged as Fort William prepared to celebrate. The ceremony, perhaps

The controversial seawall, Fort William – footpath and signal box; level crossing in the background. (J. L. Stevenson Collection)

fortunately, would not be held at the controversial station. With platforms and canopies in place but otherwise unfinished, it was left to the scheduled trains which had begun four days earlier.

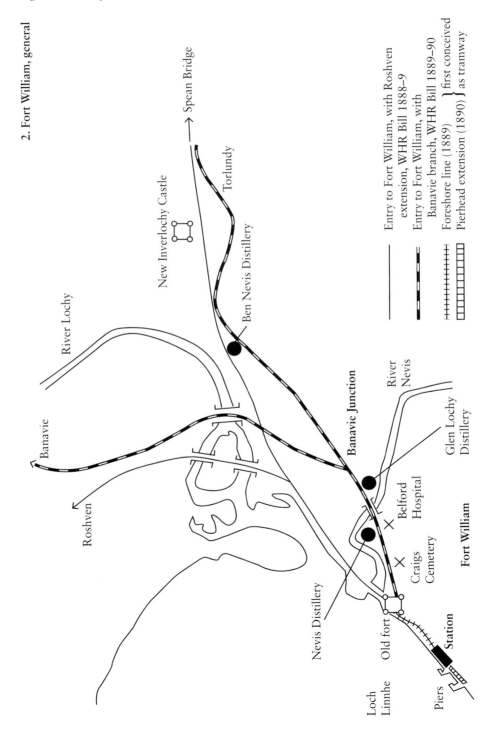

2. Fort William, general

Entry to Fort William, with Roshven extension, WHR Bill 1888–9

Entry to Fort William, with Banavie branch, WHR Bill 1889–90

Foreshore line (1889) } first conceived
Pierhead extension (1890) } as tramway

Chapter 5

The District Superintendent

Mr William Arnott, Station Agent at Perth, to be District Superintendent of the West Highland north of Ardlui.

North British Railway minutes, 21 June 1894

Arnott's appointment acknowledged the distinctive character of the 100-mile West Highland line and the independence (nominal though this was) of the West Highland Company. His salary was set at £250 per annum and he enjoyed the courtesy, conventional in the railway industry, of a free pass over neighbouring systems. Arnott arrived in Lochaber a stranger, carrying more than a hint of North British imperialism. Perth, where the North British shared the General Station, was a railway frontier and Fort William another frontier posting. On-the-spot operating experience of an untried and isolated route was desirable. However, Arnott would be expected, in addition, to keep a wary eye on the activities of the Caledonian and Highland companies, both still smarting at North British penetration of the western Highlands.

The forceful secretary-manager of the Callander & Oban Railway was not to be Arnott's model. John Anderson had known lean times, when Caledonian support was grudging; in his Oban office he could reflect on hard-won success, while noting the evident desire of the North British to invade his territory. The Caledonian now allowed him a wide freedom. Arnott, though proudly conscious of his new status, had no comparable vice-regal ambitions. He was assiduously loyal to his company, and his wordy, sometimes self-serving, reports to North British headquarters may have wearied the able and urbane John Conacher. Nevertheless, the West Highland's earliest years are well recorded in the new district superintendent's heavy longhand.

Arnott attended Major Marindin's July inspection, when the line was declared unready. Taking his tone from Conacher, he was inclined to blame Charles Forman. Thereafter, relations between the two remained uneasy. Taxed with too-optimistic forecasts, the engineer had retorted that all was conditional on weather and circumstances, while contractors Lucas & Aird complained that they had been pressured, against their better judgement, to hasten the work in adverse conditions. Opening that summer was a very near thing, and, with everything inessential put

William Arnott. (Department of Transport/NRS)

on hold, Arnott faced many problems. That the Board of Trade might uphold Fort William's appeal against railway occupation of the foreshore was his prime concern. If Marindin ruled against the pierhead station, there must be other passenger provision until a permanent answer could be found; and Arnott planned to adapt the temporary platform prepared for opening day.

Fort William station, West Highland Railway, *c.* 1945 – little changed externally after fifty years. (H. C. Casserley collection)

The foreshore dispute was far from over. With right of access through the station not yet formally established, boatmen and fishermen continued to make their way along the line (trespassing, as Arnott saw it) to the jetties abutting the seawall. Marindin's verdict at least ensured that the station need not be remodelled. From the two dead-end bays there opened a modest concourse enclosed by the main building, which (like so much else) was only completed months later. Meanwhile, the internal layout demanded attention. Arnott thought the urinal unseemly, positioned starkly at the bay ends, and banished it to the detached town-side range. Refreshment rooms, he insisted, were indispensable: 'People coming by boat and taking the long train journey will require them.' Several parties sought the lease, and Joseph Stewart of the Royal Hotel, Tyndrum, was the successful bidder. Outside, the abrupt rise to Fort William High Street was objectionable and tested horses severely.[1] Under Arnott's prodding, by January 1895 Lucas & Aird had eased the gradient and marked out a carriage stance at the station's pierhead entrance.

The seaside through road was looped, once across the pierhead, which allowed the engine of an arriving train to draw forward, run round and, tender-first, return the empty stock to the station. A crossover gave release from the bay roads. This was provision enough for the standard passenger sets, but lengthy trains could not

Fort William station, West Highland Railway – concourse, *c.* 1970. The roof and roof lights were its best features. (RCAHMS/ Courtesy of John R. Hume)

clear the points at the station throat, where the three roads merged into the single main. The well-patronised specials of September and October 1894, introducing excursionists to the West Highland, needed eight coaches or more. These extras were split outside the station limits on arrival and pieced together for departure, which claimed two platforms and interrupted other movements. It was all a foretaste of West Highland summers to come. No stock was gangwayed at this date, and coaches standing beyond the station limits were inaccessible. Flustered or impatient passengers risked injury, attempting to alight or board. As the evenings drew in and the last excursions left in the gloaming, Arnott increasingly feared such an incident.[2]

There was just room to lengthen the platforms a little, but no possibility of handling horse-and-carriage traffic, still an important adjunct of First Class passenger business. Carriage trucks and horse boxes were loaded and unloaded at the skimpy bank in the old fort goods yard, which caused Arnott much anxiety. Delays were inevitable, hazards greater: a horse injured, a barouche damaged, was sure to antagonise influential persons. Of First Class passengers and accoutrements transferring between rail and sea at Fort William there is little evidence, despite the promoters' expectations; but the Lochaber proprietors who went south for the London season

North British Railway 4-4-0T at Fort William. These diminuitive locomotives served the West Highland Railway's Banavie branch and (from 1907) the Invergarry & Fort Augustus Railway. (J. Alsop collection)

welcomed the convenience of the West Highland. Cameron of Lochiel was one such. Since 1880 he had sent his equipage by the Callander & Oban, and in May of 1894 he requested this arrangement 'one last time' (John Anderson received a personal letter of thanks, in Lochiel's best patrician tones).

The second week of public traffic brought heavy rainfall. Early on 14 August the Inverlair signalman reported that the embankment leading to the Laggan viaduct had shifted. Arnott, quickly on the spot, saw the formation hastily packed. Thorough repairs were carried out the same day, without interruption to trains. A choked culvert was the culprit, 'almost identical with [what] happened at Achallader' (see Chapter 2). Other embankments were undermined, though not breached, at Inverroy and in Glen Falloch. Maintenance in the first months lay with Lucas & Aird, whose men did not always patrol ahead of the first trains. Arnott noted how, on the Callander & Oban line, the Caledonian routinely increased surveillance in bad weather: 'It might be well that this was adopted.' Some three weeks later he personally experienced a near-derailment in Glen Spean:

When travelling with the 12.42 p.m. train ex Glasgow … between the 88th and 85th mile posts, the carriage … gave such a lurch that I really thought the train was off the road and every passenger … was very much alarmed.

The track was found badly out of gauge. Formans & McCall, under pressure to finish station buildings and railwaymen's houses, were diverting the contractor's labour force from routine checks to other tasks.

Donald P. MacDonald, who had lent his name to the West Highland promotion, owned the Nevis distillery, within the burgh, and leased the Abingers' Ben Nevis

THE OLD "LONG JOHN" DISTILLERY AND BEN NEVIS.

Nevis distillery and Ben Nevis. *(Mountain, Moor and Loch)*

at Lochy Bridge. He had been promised sidings on the Torlundy–Fort William deviation. The new Glen Lochy distillery, independent of MacDonald, was built just east of the Nevis viaduct and began production in 1895, and it too would have a siding. All three connections lay unfinished. Fort William's 'whisky traffic' was the largest single source of goods revenue in Arnott's province, and diplomatic apologies were imperative. Connection westward by the Arisaig mail cart waited to be settled, as did coach operator Hugh MacDonald's timetable for connection with Kinlochlaggan, Newtonmore and Kingussie; stables and a turning circle were being completed at Inverlair. (The Kingussie coach service of the 1880s is a measure of the improvements which the West Highland would bring. Departure from Fort William was then at 5.30 a.m., returning at 8 p.m. – it was Lochaber's only link, save by the Caledonian Canal, to the Highland Railway. Through fares were available for the day-long journey via Perth to Edinburgh or Glasgow.)

Angus Cameron, whose business as an itinerant cattle dealer covered western Inverness-shire, seized the opportunity to become a settled auctioneer. He proposed an auction mart at Lochy Bridge, where the distillery siding could be duplicated. Weekly markets would benefit both Fort William and the West Highland Company. When the new Lord Abinger (succeeded 1892) refused to release land for an access road, the Fort William commissioners offered a site within the burgh, at Nevis Bridge.3 Here a siding could not easily be given. Arnott agreed, with misgivings, that herding to and from the goods yard be tried. Sale days soon proved chaotic. There were no pens; livestock blocked the level crossing or overwhelmed the unfenced loading bank and shepherds' collies pursued escaping sheep among the sidings.

The engine depot and general yard were hemmed in by the old fort walls. (To include the passenger station, even on the landward side levelled by Lucas & Aird, would have been a tight fit – c.f. today's station approximately on this site and opened in 1975 after freight handling and locomotive servicing had moved out of town to Tomnafaire depot.) From the yard loop, which conformed to the curve of the main line, a dead end paralleled the main and reached to Nevis distillery. This served as head shunt for the locomotive roads, coaling stage and yard sidings. Operating practice allowed exit from the loop in the direction of Banavie Junction; an arriving goods normally went down the seawall, surrendered the final tablet at the signal box and backed to the yard. Arnott found the engine shed ready, but little else. Though Cameron & Co., the carters accredited by the North British, had provided a horse lorry for local deliveries and uplifts, there was at first 'no loading bank, crane [or] weigh bridge'. Goods traffic could not be handled efficiently – if indeed it could be handled at all. The open sidings would suffice for coal, minerals and other bulk consignments; van traffic needed covered accommodation, and the goods shed had not been begun.

Before August ended, Arnott reported that he must refuse heavy consignments 'for want of appliances'. A retiring room (provided for the opening day banquet) served as the goods office for several weeks, without a fireplace or stove. Blown down in an

TULLOCH and KINGUSSIE

(ROYAL ROUTE *via* LOCH LAGGAN),

AND IN CONNECTION WITH

West Highland Railway, Tulloch; Highland Railway, Kingussie.

THESE well-appointed Four-in-Hand Coaches leave Tulloch Station daily (Sundays excepted) at 7.10 and 11.30 A.M., in connection with the 6.20 and 10.25 A.M. Trains from Fort William, arriving at Kingussie at 11.50 A.M. and 4.30 P.M. Leaving Kingussie at 9.15 A.M. and 1.15 P.M., arriving at Tulloch at 3.30 and 5.45 P.M.; thence Train to Fort William.

Fares from Tulloch Station to Kingussie, 12s. 6d. each.

(Coachman's Fees not included.)

NOTE.—Parties wishing to have Private Carriages to Loch Laggan and to the Shooting Lodges on the route and to Kingussie, and *vice versa*, can be arranged for at Coach Office, Fort William and Kingussie, and at Tulloch Station, West Highland Railway.

HUGH M'DONALD,

Coach Proprietor.

TELEGRAPHIC ADDRESS:
"COACH OFFICE, FORT WILLIAM."

Notice, Tulloch–Kingussie coach service, 1897. (Author's collection)

October gale, it was replaced by the temporary ticket office from Inverlair, where the station building was now finished. Siding accommodation overall was insufficient. The distillery tracks, unballasted and insecure, were used to stable empty excursion stock – an expedient which could not continue. Wagons of non-perishable goods were held at Spean Bridge to await attention when space permitted.[4] High on Arnott's agenda, only two months after opening day, was the annual movement of sheep out of the Highlands for sale or wintering. Crofters and farmers condemned the first crude arrangements at intermediate stations and Donald MacDougall, North British goods manager, feared 'losing large traffic' unless every loading bank was ash-blinded and enclosures put in place. Arnott wanted permanent pens, citing practice at Perth: 'Hurdles cannot stand before wild Highland cattle.' But the Board of Trade required that fixed enclosures be paved, with regular, labour-intensive cleaning and disinfecting. The Callander & Oban, he discovered, relied on moveable hurdles. Though too late for that autumn, priority was given to Bridge of Orchy, where droves bound for Callander & Oban Tyndrum might be intercepted. The bank there, warned MacDougall, was scarcely usable:

> The top cover … is [still] made up of rough stones, and sheep can … force themselves through [the] wire fence ... The [farmer] who had the special … yesterday, complained bitterly of … rough handling …

By early 1895 it had been cleared of the larger rubble, blinded to a depth of several inches and enclosed by a post-and-rail fence.

3. Fort William, old fort, locomotive depot and goods yard, c.1896

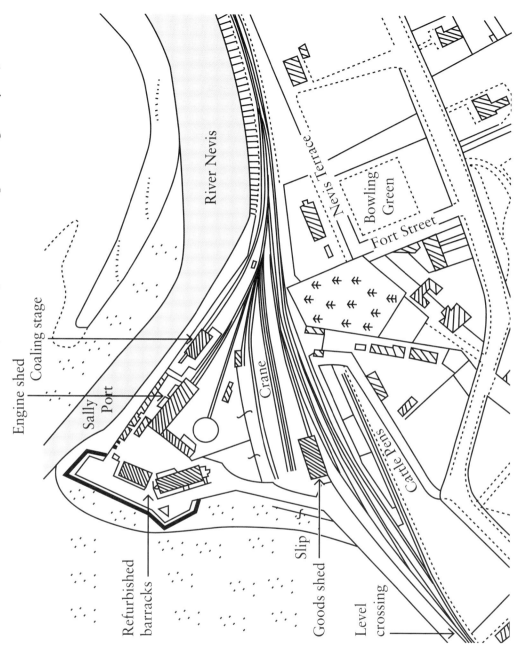

Engine shed

Coaling stage

River Nevis

Sally Port

Crane

Nevis Terrace

Bowling Green

Fort Street

Cattle Pens

Refurbished barracks

Slip

Goods shed

Level crossing

Chapter 6

Southern End and Inveraray; Crianlarich

Upper Helensburgh station, West Highland Railway, with Craigendoran–Arrochar & Tarbet local headed by North British Railway 0-4-4T (J. Alsop collection)

The West Highland increased the range of the North British Company's Glasgow residential traffic and enlarged the already elaborate pattern of summer-season excursions embracing the Trossachs, Loch Lomond and the Clyde Coast, in which Caledonian, Glasgow & South Western and North British all participated.[1] It followed that Glasgow district superintendent George Cunningham should have general charge of the West Highland south of Ardlui. Cunningham outranked William Arnott and carried more weight within the company, but they encountered similar problems (see Chapter 7). Married signalmen could not find homes to rent, even along the Gare Loch. Forced to accept that housing shortages and the cost of living made the West Highland a special case, nevertheless the North British directors maintained that, on the southern sections, 'the men do not have the same claim'.

It was first intended to introduce Glasgow–Garelochhead locals, supplementing the North British Glasgow–Balloch/Helensburgh timetable, while Glasgow–Fort William trains would run express to Garelochead – with similar provision in the up direction. A Craigendoran–Arrochar & Tarbet shuttle was soon substituted, running three or four times daily and connecting with the Glasgow–Helensburgh trains.[2] Deuchars was reluctant to drop his outer suburban strategy, and the turntable installed at Garelochhead remained there, against second thoughts. But Conacher and Wieland were convinced that the West Highland promoters had exaggerated the local traffic to be won. The new arrangement placated the Luss Trustees, who wanted Lochlongside and Glen Douglas to be better served. James Morrison, managing

Shandon Hydropathic. (J&C McCutcheon Collection)

director of Shandon Hydropathic and a West Highland promoter, much disliked the original timetable. It meant change of train – at Glasgow for his Edinburgh and south-of-the-Border guests, at Garelochhead for those making a day excursion along the new railway. Fort William services, including the West Highland's overnight 'English portion', soon became more-or-less 'all stations' and called at Shandon.[3]

Whistlefield and Portincaple

Above Portincaple on Loch Long, opposite Loch Goil, the promised station at Whistlefield had not been built. The Colquhouns' displeasure – they complained that their Glen Mallan lodge could not be let – and the pressure of a local campaign brought West Highland and North British to fulfil their obligation. Weekend or seasonal 'residenters' [sic] argued that daily commuting would increase when a platform was provided. They pointed to the summer visitors who drove, or came on foot, from the Gare Loch steamers. Whistlefield was a popular destination for

Whistlefield station, West Highland Railway, looking to Loch Goil. (Lens of Sutton Collection)

Sunday school picnic parties and for delicate city dwellers in search of bracing air. Fishermen claimed that by landing at Portincaple they could relieve congestion in these narrow waters, cart more cheaply to the railway – Arrochar & Tarbet station was some distance from Arrochar pier – and catch earlier markets on Clydeside. Goods manager MacDougall advised that a coal and general-purposes siding at Whistlefield might pay for itself, because the steep road from Garelochhead limited carters' loads. Station and siding were in use from October 1896. The gradient, rising towards Glen Douglas, demanded strict adherence to operating rules.

Conacher was badgered throughout 1894–6 to entertain a funicular railway from Whistlefield to Portincaple, linking West Highland trains with a dedicated steamer for Loch Goil. Glasgow solicitor J.M. Taylor repeatedly attempted to advance the scheme. At their first meeting he was accompanied by Charles Forman, who had planned the 2-mile line. Thereafter the general manager played for time: he replied to one enquirer that assessment of the Portincaple project must precede any decision on a station for Whistlefield, to another that the funicular could not be considered until Whistlefield station was ready. Taylor's several formulae for the division of Glasgow–Loch Goil revenues and working expenses were all in the end rejected. However, Conacher trod warily. The well-to-do householders of Carrick Castle, Douglas Pier and Lochgoilhead were not without influence, and one of them, writing in Taylor's support, hinted of his friends among the North British directors. By contrast, there was no need to entertain suggestions, seemingly short lived, for a conventional branch from the West Highland down the Rosneath peninsula.

South Argyll

Though the Loch Fyne Light Railway, authorised in 1897, seems a West Highland afterthought, it had a remoter background. An extension of the busy Glasgow–Helensburgh line (completed in 1858 and in North British hands from 1865) had been proposed more than once. The intention was, on the face of things, innocently local. Encouraging residential business, a railway along the Gare Loch, perhaps continuing to Loch Long, would complement the steamers (cf. Taylor's scheme, above). But from 1880, with the Callander & Oban Railway completed westward from Tyndrum, the Caledonian Company had reason to be suspicious. Arrochar, at the head of Loch Long, might become a railhead for Inveraray and Loch Fyne, rivalling Callander & Oban Dalmally. Strategic calculation intensified when Caledonian and North British came to weigh up the opportunities and risks of a Glasgow–Crianlarich cut-off (see Chapter 1).The Caledonian had been well aware how first Garelochhead and then Arrochar might lead their enemy on to Crianlarich.

With the West Highland in being, the landowners and farmers of South Argyll, who looked east to the markets and wintering grounds of Perthshire and Stirlingshire, sought escape from dependence on water transport and transhipment at Glasgow.

Their priority was agricultural traffic, to pass between West Highland and Callander & Oban by the Crianlarich spur. Loch Fyne could be left to the steamers, but fish too might go eastward via Crianlarich. To these ends, their preference was an Ardlui–Inveraray branch via Glen Kinglas, despite engineering costs. They possessed the resources to commission their own survey and could not be ignored. The North British proposed instead, when the impending light railways legislation was in place, a line from Arrochar & Tarbet by Glen Croe, over Rest-and-be-Thankful, terminating at St Catherine's on Loch Fyne, opposite Inveraray.

John Anderson's riposte, endorsed by the Caledonian, was a conventional Dalmally–Inveraray branch, engineered by Forman. It would afford the desired easterly outlet. In an interview with the Duke of Argyll, Anderson explained that he must forestall 'our friends over the hill'. However, the ducal family were already well disposed to the North British (see Chapter 9). The inconvenience of a ferry notwithstanding, they favoured the West Highland option, leaving 'their town' (and their private policies) uninvaded. Elsewhere in the county, there was still resentment that the North British had abandoned the Clyde, Ardrishaig & Crinan (see Chapter 1). In consequence, the Dalmally scheme, included in the composite Callander & Oban Bill of 1896/7, did not lack support.[4] But it was defeated, while the Loch Fyne Light Railway was never begun. South Argyll had been accounted prime territory for light construction – perhaps continuing from St Catherine's to Dunoon, perhaps from Inveraray down into Kintyre. But enthusiasm soon ebbed – an early indication that the 1896 Light Railways Act, of which much was expected, would produce at best patchy results.[5]

Crianlarich

On the Callander & Oban, Crianlarich was an intermediate station of no special significance. West Highland Crianlarich, some 35 miles from Craigendoran but halfway between Glasgow and Fort William, became a place of importance. Though William Arnott held administrative command, the North British engineering and locomotive departments loomed large. Here, a ballast squad were based; here, invariably, locomotives were watered and their fires tended.[6] With the servicing interval for each passenger train prominently displayed, Crianlarich's 'dining room', on the island platform between chalet building and signal box, did a steady trade (it remains today, in café guise). Food baskets could be pre-ordered by telegraph, which overnight travellers from England quickly appreciated. (Restaurant and buffet cars waited till the 1920s, to be received in certain quarters with austere Presbyterian disapproval. O. S. Nock records an encounter with an old shepherd, aghast at the idea of 'eating and drinking on a railway train'.)

Opposite: West Highland Railway Bill, 1888/9, Formans & McCall's estimate for Crainlarich spur ('Railway No. 4'). (Author's collection)

4   .

WEST HIGHLAND RAILWAY.

Crianlarich Junction.

Estimate for the proposed Railways—*continued.*

Railway No. 4.	Miles.	f.	chs.	Whether Single or Double.
Length of Line	0	5	5·7	Single.

	Cubic yards.	Price per yd. s. d.	£ s. d.	£ s. d.
Earthworks :—				
Cuttings—Rock				
Soft Soil ..	20,724	0 10	863 10 0	
Roads	500	1 0	25 0 0	
TOTAL ..	21,224	..	888 10 0	888 10 0
Embankments, including Roads .. .. 31,778 cubic yards				475 0 0
Bridges—Public Roads.. .. .. Number, 2				1,200 0 0
Accommodation Bridges and Works				250 0 0
Viaducts				
Tunnels				
Culverts and Drains				187 10 0
Metallings of Roads and Level Crossings				350 0 0
Gatekeepers' Houses at Level Crossings				

Permanent Way, including Fencing :

	MILES F. CHS.	COST PER MILE. £ s. d.	
	0 5 5·7 at	1,586 0 0	1,104 5 0
Permanent Way for Sidings, and Cost of Junctions			1,200 0 0
Stations			750 0 0
		£	6,405 5 0
Contingencies .. .. 10 per Cent.			640 10 6
		£	7,045 15 6
	A. R. P.		
Land and Buildings :	5 2 0		275 0 0
TOTAL		£	7,320 15 6

Say **£7,321 0 0**

FORMANS & McCALL,   .
Engineers.

East Coast Anglo-Scottish timetable, August 1894, showing London–Fort William through coach. (Courtesy of Scottish Railway Preservation Society)

In the West Highland's first weeks of traffic, with the Crianlarich spur unfinished and no arrangements for interchange agreed, Arnott could only ensure that luggage was transferred as required to and from the Callander & Oban trains. The West Highland access road, its gravel surface unconsolidated, was unusable for loaded barrows. This entailed a detour by the public highways. Since 1889, construction and opening of the spur had been at an impasse. The Caledonian Company challenged the design of Forman's viaduct over the Oban line, pursuing their case through the Scottish courts. Caledonian general manager James Thompson next proposed joint station arrangements, elaborately (and expensively) laid out across Fillan Water, for through running in all directions – an answer ostensibly in the spirit of the two companies' New Lines Agreement (see Chapter 3). The North British rightly suspected delaying tactics. Moreover, Thompson's plan might presage a Caledonian bid for running powers to Fort William and a share in the Mallaig Extension – a most unwelcome complication whether seriously pressed or not (see Chapter 10). Any lingering North British hopes of access to Oban in their own right were best forgotten in case the Caledonian sought a Crianlarich–Fort William quid pro quo.

A simpler option was to site the West Highland station on the curve approaching the contested viaduct, above a re-sited Callander & Oban station, so that passenger exchange could be effected by ramps and stairs. However, the linking spur would

Crianlarich station: chalet building, 'dining room', water tanks, and railwaymen's tenement; West Highland Railway. (J. L. Stevenson Collection)

have lain awkwardly, touching neither station. The Caledonian were unimpressed – and Thompson refused a review of all extant Caledonian–North British exchange arrangements, as prelude to a general treaty including Crianlarich. Attention returned to the details of the spur as first surveyed by Forman and an arbiter of standing, engineer Sir Douglas Galton, was nominated by the Board of Trade. His award effectively settled the matter, but the Caledonian made new difficulties over the layout of the lower (i.e. Callander & Oban) junction and demanded that the spur be worked by a shunting pilot, entirely at North British expense.

Lord Breadalbane's farm tenants in Glen Falloch and Glen Orchy, like their counterparts in the districts around Loch Fyne, looked for easier access via Crianlarich to the markets of Perthshire and Stirlingshire. Glen Dochart and Strathfillan, already served by the Callander & Oban, welcomed the shorter West Highland route to Glasgow. Until the spur came into use, these expectations could not be fully realised. Anderson's experience told him that the West Highland promoters had exaggerated the traffic in question; however, such as it was, the Callander & Oban would gain something, and he urged Thompson to cease obstruction. Conacher and his deputy were privately of

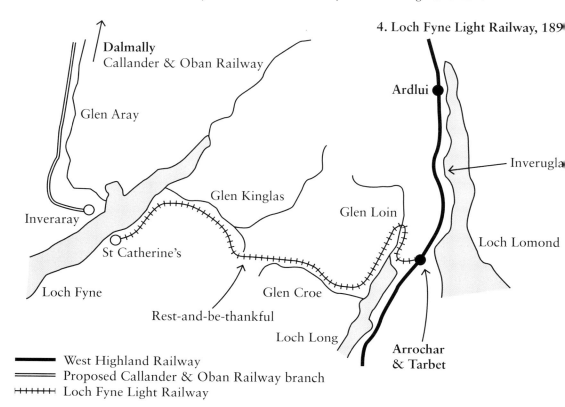

4. Loch Fyne Light Railway, 189

Anderson's opinion – little revenue was in prospect, and Deuchars recommended that the spur be left in limbo 'as long as we can keep it closed'. The exchange of wagon traffic might be marginally worthwhile if the Caledonian agreed, as in the end they did, that the engines of the regular Callander & Oban and West Highland goods trains might shunt up and down the spur. Neither Caledonian nor North British really wanted regular passenger interchange. The link at last came into use in 1897; but the two routes continued distinct.7 The upper (i.e. West Highland) junction was kept simple. It was overlooked by the signal box, a squat version of the standard North British article. Dwarf signal cabins were standard at all the other intermediate West Highland stations – except Row (Rhu), where siting required a taller structure.

Chapter 7

Early Days

The popularity of West Highland excursions in the late summer and autumn of 1894 left the line's tourist potential in no doubt. There were also 'guaranteed trains' – specials block-booked by various organisations eager to sample the new route, for example the Dumbarton Traders' Association. The first Glasgow–Fort William day-trip was advertised for Saturday 25 August. It ran ahead of the early scheduled train north and followed the last scheduled train south. Tickets were available from every station between Bridgeton Cross and Hyndland on the Glasgow City & District Railway (a North British subsidiary). On Friday 31st, the first special *from* Fort William took 350 Cameron Volunteers (some joining at Spean Bridge and Roy Bridge) to a grand review at Craigendoran. On Edinburgh's autumn holiday, the North British offered a Fort William outing, with a 6.30 a.m. departure. A September excursion allowed city exiles to attend the Lochaber Highland Games, an important date in Fort William's calendar. When yet another Glasgow–Fort William special was offered, demand justified a duplicate. Both trains were loaded to capacity, and, by one account, remarshalled into *three* return workings, which must have tested the ingenuity of district superintendent Arnott. Throughout October, despite the shortening light, North British stations across the Central Belt offered cheap Saturday afternoon tickets to West Highland stations as far as Ardlui.

After a fortnight of regular traffic, drivers began to report 'bad curves' where previously their engines rode well. A rainy autumn called for vigilance where any earthworks were suspect, and trackside drains needed repeated attention. Many lesser culverts had been displaced or broken under the heavy ballast trains and replacement continued. For day-to-day maintenance the contractors' men were, in Arnott's opinion, poorly skilled, insufficiently alert, inadequately supervised and too thinly spread. Driver Stirling complained that the Fort William squad who patrolled to Rannoch often neglected 'putting their flag out at the proper distance'. A Glasgow–Garelochhead local was derailed near Upper Helensburgh – by the large stone deliberately placed on the rails by a teenage delinquent. There were no injuries and the overturned tank engine was quickly recovered, but the incident revealed, to the alarm of North British engineer James Carswell, how Lucas & Aird's gangs lacked proper tools, while 'none of the Contractor's officials were about'.

James Bell (Carswell's deputy and eventual successor) found that 'the road was very much out of line and level' between Achallader and Lochtreighead. Imposing a 20 mph limit in Strathtulla, and 15 mph on Rannoch Moor, he assigned three traffic inspectors to oversee the travelling squads. All the contractor's foremen must be given flags, lamps, working timetables and notice of additional trains. Assured by Lucas & Aird that henceforth the cess all across the Moor would be inspected daily, and more often during heavy rain, Bell permitted the resumption of timetable speed. Formans & McCall remained ultimately answerable, and Charles Forman was ready to contest North British fault-finding:

> Looking to its length [and] the ... amount of traffic sent over it ... the line is in remarkably good order.

The West Highland, he repeated, was brought into use at the earliest possible moment, as the North British demanded. During July and August he had ensured that every culvert between Crianlarich and Fort William vulnerable to flooding was more generously proportioned; if not for the labour dispute which had interrupted the supply of pipes, the entire route would have been covered. As for the contractor's shortcomings, the North British had been niggardly in issuing jacks, lifting screws and even oil cans and fish-plate oil. No warning detonators were available. Forman especially challenged Arnott's strictures. Going over the line in early September, just as Bell had done, he had noted 'all the surfacemen at their posts and a very marked improvement in the road'. On the moorland sections (Gortan–Rannoch and Rannoch–Corrour) consolidation would be hastened, which Bell conceded, by steady running at a moderate speed, left to the enginemen's judgement.

North from Glen Douglas, where the line was terraced high above Loch Long, minor rock falls persisted. Buttresses and patches supplemented the retaining walls, yet Bell, aware of Callander & Oban experience in Glen Ogle and the Pass of Brander, feared for a time that an expensive safety system would be needed. On this stretch of line and at other locations, he prescribed additional check rails. Forman concurred; all 'outside' curves of less than 15 chains radius ought to be treated. (On 'inside' bends, a derailed engine would come to rest against the mountainside; on 'outside' bends a headlong plunge was not impossible.) Marindin had criticised the worst reverse curves, recommending that short lengths of straight be inserted, which Forman had begun. Bell would persevere and abrupt curvature was, as far as possible, eliminated. Additional sleepers per rail length were also added. By 1900, the West Highland permanent way would be altogether more substantial.[1]

West Highland secretary George Wieland was the company's only real executive figure. He came to believe, as did John Conacher, that time and money could be saved if Carswell took over both outstanding work and routine upkeep – the latter conventionally left to the contractor during the first year of traffic. They were mindful of Marindin's understated warning that the West Highland needed 'a lot of watching'.

The Board of Trade would not tolerate indefinitely Lucas & Aird's indiscriminate practice, with ballast squads, patrol men and other workers travelling daily from Craigendoran, Crianlarich and Fort William. Surfacemen with regular beats ought to be resident along the route, and Conacher expected their cottages to have priority. On his September visit, Bell saw only eight lineside houses in progress – at Shandon, Whistlefield and Milepost 16; then, further north, at Lochtreighead, Fersit, Monessie, Spean Bridge and Auchindaul. Bricks had been delivered to the other sites settled with Forman, but completion before winter was unlikely, especially on Rannoch Moor where the need was greatest.

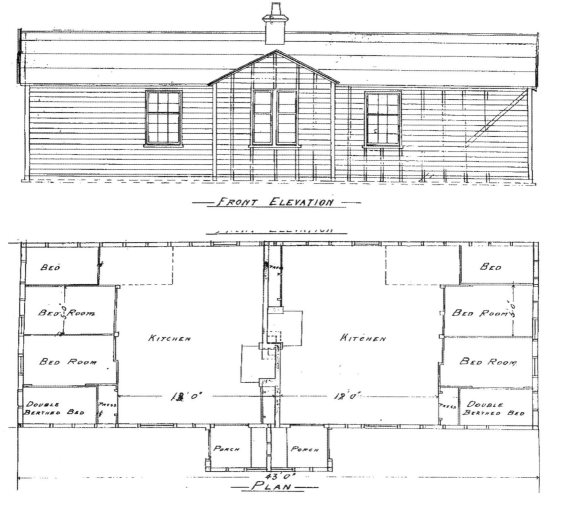

North British Railway, surfacemen's temporary cottages for West Highland Railway. (Author's collection)

Losing patience, Conacher insisted that the North British take direct control. A compromise was negotiated, effective from October 1894. Lucas & Aird would finish the stationmasters' cottages already in progress. They would complete the Banavie branch, for which they still had plant in situ, also finishing Fort William station and the Nevis distillery sidings. They would build the short road from station to Hydropathic at Shandon, and the screening wall at Upper Helensburgh, where householders complained of lost amenity. For all else Carswell assumed responsibility, and the travelling squads joined the North British payroll. Bowing to this arrangement, Forman predicted (accurately) that Carswell's department would find themselves overstretched; he added (again, accurately) that, in negotiating with painters and other tradesmen subcontracted to Lucas & Aird, the North British would meet with more delays. From the years of construction, large huts were still scattered along the route, having served as dormitories, mess rooms, on-site offices and stores, but these were too decrepit and grubby after five winters to be turned into temporary housing. Instead, Carswell planned 'double' wooden cottages until all his surfacemen could occupy permanent family dwellings. Conacher wanted 'increased bedroom accommodation', which brought the price of each 'double' to £170, but indicated that Carswell might economise on piped water and sewerage. North of Garelochhead no local authority interference need be expected, except within the burgh boundaries of Fort William.

It had been intended that at intermediate stations along the route only stationmasters should have company houses. Signalmen, married or single, must seek their own accommodation. (Tyndrum and Bridge of Orchy began with 'agent and lad-porter', the former qualified in single-line tablet operation.) But, as Arnott put it: 'Married men would … be more contented in that part of the country [where] it is difficult … to find lodgings.' Conacher and the North British board were persuaded to authorise cottages. Deuchars was soon besieged by all the traffic department men who transferred to Fort William: 'Besides the Signalman … difficulty has been experienced in finding houses for two Passenger Guards, one Inspector and one Clerk.' The engine drivers and firemen now based at Fort William shed petitioned locomotive superintendent Matthew Holmes:

> We … beg to draw your special attention as regards house accommodation, winter approaching and no signs [sic] of a house neither temporary nor permanent We would beseech you to take this matter up.
>   Jas Kay, Alex Williamson, Archibald Stirling, Wm Clarkson, Thos Wilson, Robt Beattie

Lucas & Aird had leased a villa adjacent to their Fort William base on the understanding that it would become available to the North British superintendent. With the Banavie branch to complete, they kept possession into 1895, and Arnott, obliged to take a larger house, feared that he would be 'worse off than when in Perth' – until the North British increased his salary and purchased the property outright.[2]

Glen Douglas passing place – signal box with cottage and platform for local trains. (Lens of Sutton Collection)

Carswell concentrated, as ordered, on his own surfacemen, besides passenger facilities. Other houses, already neglected in the final push to open the West Highland, received only hit and miss attention during the latter part of 1894. By the turn of the year some were half built; others, though more or less ready, lacked roughcast. As for internal fittings, the various subcontractors had downed tools until assured that the North British would honour the terms which Lucas & Aird had agreed. Plasterwork (both external and internal), ruined by the first frosts, could not be redone until the spring. The station buildings were at least weatherproof and equipped with fireplaces, and in several instances stationmasters and signalmen chose to camp out in waiting rooms, little guessing that this makeshift arrangement would continue for many months.

Glen Douglas, Gortan and Corrour passing places had conventional signal boxes with cottages attached. By November 1894 these little houses held railway families. Damp courses had been omitted and the gables were unharled. In December a traffic inspector branded the Corrour cottage 'disgraceful'; that at Gortan he found 'pleasant by comparison', but both were extremely dank. Rain penetrated the wind-lashed signal boxes, which lacked porches. As New Year 1895 approached, the despairing Corrour signalman registered his 'last complaint' to Arnott:

Impossible to keep the instruments in working order … I am standing in three inches of water…

Chapter 8

Snow

Snow, Rannoch Moor, *c.* 1950. (J. L. Stevenson Collection)

Several places were identified where trouble might be expected, especially Cruach cutting. However, the winters of 1892/3 and 1893/4 had been wet and stormy, with less than average snow, and the North British Company wanted operating experience before committing to protection measures. Just five months open, the West Highland was poorly prepared for the arctic conditions that marked the first months of 1895 across much of Scotland. Matthew Holmes planned to employ the heaviest North

British 0-6-0s. Having proved themselves during the final year of construction (see Chapter 2), these locomotives were given goods and ballast duties when the line opened. As plough engines, despatched from either end of the route when snow was reported, they would meet on Rannoch Moor and, coupled tender-to-tender, work back and forth as required. When they parted company, the Cowlairs (Glasgow) plough might continue to Fort William, the Fort William plough to Cowlairs.[1] By exchanging engines, the two crews could return home without the hazards of running tender-first through driving snow.

The North British ploughs were, by the latest standards, old-fashioned, to the disquiet of Charles Forman:

> The Highland Company use steel ploughs shaped so as to lift and throw the snow clear. The plough I saw at Fort William … seemed to be wooden with a square-up end like the bow of a ship.

Holmes's strategy was, he thought, too rigid. What if blizzard conditions were encountered en route to the Rannoch rendezvous? Two ploughs should be mounted, fore and aft, on each engine, giving a better chance of escape from impenetrable drifts. That there was no turntable in the 90 miles between Garelochhead and Fort William necessitated a more flexible response. No water was available between Bridge of Orchy and Inverlair (to be renamed Tulloch during 1895); when standing time alternated with arduous ploughing, reserves were soon depleted. And the Rannoch 'meet' might come too late. Despatching the ploughs in good time, before snow accumulated, could make all the difference. Overnight drifting meant an altogether tougher task the next morning; but, with so many stationmasters' houses unfinished or unoccupied, there was no ready means of opening up the line at night, after the last scheduled trains had passed.

A moderate snowfall saw in the New Year and confirmed Cruach as a trouble-spot:

> It being so narrow, the wreaths [drifts] formed a wall the width of the plough, and in the event of a … protracted storm the cutting would get entirely choked up. [Arnott's report]

The district superintendent urged that snow fences be erected at once: better still, the cutting might be roofed. The alternative, he suggested, was to widen it, which might produce marketable granite to offset the cost of excavation. There was no time for any remedy. In the early morning of Monday 7 January snow steadily took hold, from Brae Lochaber south to Lochlomondside:

Telegrams (Arnott to Deuchars)
Monday
1. Snow plough from Fort William stuck in heavy wreath of snow near Tulloch, fourteen feet deep; other heavy wreaths southwards; no passage today.

2. 7.30 a.m. passenger ex Fort William standing at Roy Bridge.

3. 5 a.m. goods ex Sighthill (Glasgow) stuck between Ardlui and Crianlarich.

4. 7.30 a.m. train still standing at Roy Bridge. Snow plough is covered over and engine fire out; men had to retreat; no improvement.

5. Trains from Fort William cannot go beyond Roy Bridge and trains from Glasgow cannot get beyond Ardlui.

<u>Tuesday</u>

1. Snow plough through to Tulloch at 10.30 a.m.

3. Line clear south of Rannoch [Moor].

When the Cowlairs plough and supporting surfacemen reached Rannoch station that Tuesday, ahead were 'two miles of snow about twelve feet deep'. Already once derailed but restored with jacks, the engine battled into Cruach cutting, only to burst the track where the drift was immovable: 'Men exhausted; ten hours needed to clear line and eight hours to deal with snow plough engine.' The Fort William squad having reached Corrour, on Wednesday the cutting was tackled from both ends:

> The … ploughs were of little use and the snow, which was firmly welded, had all to be shovelled out by the surfacemen, which took them from two to three casts – one man at the bottom throwing it about half way up, the second man throwing it on the top, and the third man throwing it clear. Had [they] been able to face the wind, the road might have been somewhat sooner cleared. The cutting … is now full of snow, with only as much room as allows a train to clear, and if another storm or a rapid thaw comes I would be much afraid of the consequences. [Arnott's report]

Holmes and engineer Carswell wanted the Garelochhead turntable moved to Crianlarich and a plough engine kept there. Traffic superintendent Deuchars argued that an additional plough at Crianlarich would suffice, to be mounted on the ballast locomotive when need arose. He endorsed Arnott's plans for snow fences at 'two miles through Tulloch to the Laggan viaduct', 'top of Loch Treig to Corrour', and of course Cruach. While Conacher pondered his subordinates' advice, the West Highland was once more threatened. On Saturday 12 January the Crianlarich ballast train had to be dug out from wind-blown lying snow near Gortan, which delayed the morning up passenger for an hour. Next day came a new and severe blizzard.

Arnott sent out his plough, with the Fort William ballast squad in support. Reaching Corrour, they learned that Cruach cutting was already filled by a mixture of old and new snow. The Crianlarich ballast, coming north to meet them, had found the line impassable beyond Tyndrum. In failing light, both teams retreated. The Cowlairs plough was made ready that Sunday evening: 'Engine No. 645 fitted with snow plough and Engine No. 663 assisting left … about 10.40 p.m.'. The storm had moved south, and overnight the Crianlarich ballast engine was snowed in. Attempting to release it, both plough engines left the track. On Monday morning the

Fort William plough, making a second attempt, found 'wreaths of snow ten to twenty foot deep' at Lochtreighead; in the biting wind, 'the men could not stand out' and at noon work was again abandoned. They fared better on Tuesday 15th and pressed on into Rannoch Moor. Meanwhile the Cowlairs plough, back in action after Monday morning's derailment, had passed Gortan. The final miles to and through Cruach cutting were cleared that night, but not before the Fort William plough engine was derailed in turn, 'charging drifts south of Corrour'.

Debate continued. As Arnott had discovered, snow could accumulate rapidly in Glen Spean and on Lochtreigside. The Fort William ballast, running ahead of the first up passenger, risked being shut in on Rannoch Moor. Though available from late January, Crianlarich's spare plough was of little use if the men and their locomotive were 20 miles distant, performing other tasks and caught by a sudden change in the weather. A second engine might be based at Crianlarich, with a plough already mounted, but who was to raise steam? To have another driver and fireman there, with no other duties, was out of the question. Inter-departmental friction entered. Arnott, though in overall charge at Fort William, was 'traffic' and subordinate to Deuchars. The ballast squads were the engineer's, answerable to Carswell. The locomotive foreman at Fort William, with a handful of 0-6-0s and passenger 4-4-0s to meet every demand, was ultimately accountable to Holmes. Carswell complained that in the first emergency Arnott had been too hasty – sent ahead of the ballast, the Fort William plough engine was overwhelmed, with no surfacemen to dig it out (above). Forman, whose opinion was sought, took the opposite view – Arnott had been dilatory and might have taken warning before drifting became severe.

Early February brought a third daunting test when five days were required to restore scheduled services, as Arnott subsequently described:

About noon on Wednesday 6th a storm ... from the north-east ... broke out in the Lochaber and Rannoch districts. Drifting ... was very rapid, and the cuttings, which were ... all more or less full of old snow, soon got choked up. The plough was sent from Fort William ... but Inspector Campbell, of Permanent Way, and Loco Foreman Ewing, who accompanied it, decided not to proceed. The chances of getting back were very doubtful, as they had no workmen, who had left for Rannoch in the morning.

I wired Cowlairs to send a squad, who manned the Crianlarich plough. They encountered several heavy wreaths from Tyndrum on to Rannoch, reached at 2 p.m. on Thursday, when the water in the engine tanks was exhausted.[2] The Fort William plough left again at 6.30 a.m. that day, but the engine, tender and van were all derailed about half way up Loch Treig. The engine was within an ace of going over the embankment but luckily the heel of the plough slipper caught the rail and saved it.

The wind grew very high ... into Friday, and what progress [had been] made ... was filled up [sic]. By Saturday the wind had fallen, and by 3.30 p.m. on Sunday the line was clear ... This storm was more severe than those previously, with very heavy drifting in the Gortan district and on towards Bridge of Orchy. It was very bad from the top of

Loch Treig to Corrour, and Cruach Cutting was again … filled. All the cuttings are now brimful. With every storm, it becomes more arduous to clear the way. [Arnott's report]

But the worst was now over. Snow fencing could be put in hand, where needed, all the way north from Tyndrum to Glen Spean. Before the following winter Crianlarich had a turntable and engine shed. (The altered layout was approved by the Board of Trade.) Another turntable would be added at Rannoch. (The turntable pit, excavated from the peat hags around the station, can still be identified. At Crianlarich alterations have removed all vestiges of the turntable, though the shed remains in use as engineer's workshop.) From 1896, when every stationmaster along the West Highland was properly resident, an emergency procedure was established, to endure unchanged into the 1970s. The cottages had call-out bells and the circuit included an inspector's house in Fort William. When a plug-in switch, connecting with the tablet telegraph, was activated each night, every stationmaster could alert his colleagues in both directions:

Depress the tablet instrument plunger for 3 or 4 seconds at a time, repeating the signal at short intervals until answered, then communicate by telephone.

Cruach snow shed, northern end, West Highland Railway. (J. Alsop collection)

Additional water columns were authorised during 1895 (see Chapter 13). Because Rannoch was not included, Carswell protested several times:

> Our ballast trains are subject to great delays owing to there being no water for the engines and they having [sic] to run to Bridge of Orchy or Tulloch.

Though the snows were moderate, the West Highland's second winter amply reinforced the point. The engineer eventually improvised a tank and water column from a redundant boiler plus pipes left behind by Lucas & Aird, which cost an economical £60.3 More expensive was protection for Cruach cutting, transformed into a unique snow shed. On walls sprung from the hewn rock a superstructure of old rails was erected, clad longitudinally with corrugated iron. Damage from locomotive exhaust was lessened by removing the central portion during the summer months.

Chapter 9

The Landed Interest

The landowners' coalition behind the West Highland would always be precarious. Once the Colquhoun Trustees had committed to the scheme, the way was broadly clear from the Gare Loch to upper Loch Lomond. However, Campbell of Colgrain challenged the layout of Craigendoran Junction, while the small proprietors of Finnart (Loch Long)

Early days: West Highland Railway near Ardlui, looking north to Inverarnan and Glen Falloch. (Author's collection)

threatened objections, prompted (allegedly) by the Caledonian Company. Sir James Colquhoun (an absentee) wanted residential development between Helensburgh and Arrochar, but required that Lochlomondside remain unspoiled. Charles Forman was compelled to find a less obtrusive line, away from the water's edge. At Inveruglas bay (Craigenarden), where he had intended a shoreline causeway, the altered alignment included a handsome arched viaduct and the briefest of tunnels.[1]

Though a director of the Highland Railway, the Callander & Oban and the Caledonian, the Marquess of Breadalbane conceded that the West Highland was a desirable project and bent to the wishes of his large tenant farmers – among them William Menzies at Keilator (Crianlarich), who had been a promoter of the Glen Falloch Railway in 1887/8. Distrusting the evasive George Wieland, Breadalbane warmed to John Conacher and flourished his own practical railway knowledge. He urged that the North British, in working the West Highland, look to Highland and Caledonian experience. At Bridge of Orchy, where livestock traffic could be expected, the Marquess planned to re-establish a drove stance. (Giving tentative support to the Glen Falloch Railway, he had earlier made similar plans for Inverarnan.) Breadalbane also proposed a Temperance refreshment room for Bridge of Orchy station, in expectation that the summer-season coach route from Ballachulish to Glen Coe and Glen Etive would be extended to connect with the West Highland. Though he owned both Bridge of Orchy's lonely hotel and Inveroran inn, on the then parliamentary road, his lessees should not be encouraged to undertake summer coaching – they would lengthen the intervals at their premises so as to dispense 'intoxicating beverages'. Conacher, himself a Temperance enthusiast, no doubt took the point. In any case, the North British had fixed on Crianlarich as the West Highland's 'dining room' station (see Chapter 6).

Breadalbane's fragile neutrality allowed passage by Glen Falloch and Strathfillan (i.e. through Crianlarich and Tyndrum) into Glen Orchy. Following Strathtulla into Rannoch Moor, the West Highland skirted but did not divide Blackmount forest, which the Glasgow & North Western Railway would have severed. The Marquess obtained guarantees of compensation for disturbance to deer or damage to his salmon pools, and his agents were vigilant in re-measuring all the land taken. On the northern edge of Breadalbane's lands, Gortan would always be – even to rail travellers – the least known of the West Highland's isolated passing places. No public facilities, other than Bridge of Orchy station, were to be offered within his Blackmount preserves. Evincing paternalist concern for railway families (and fear of friction with his farm tenants at Auch and Achallader), Breadalbane subsequently complained that the North British had not consulted his factor before siting their surfacemen's cottages. And he went to law over water rights because the North British assumed, too casually, that they might tap or divert a mountain stream some distance from Bridge of Orchy, where a water column was essential.

Sir Robert Menzies of Weem, whose lands stretched west to Loch Laidon and the River Gauer, became a promoter. He was eager for another railhead, additional to

Gortan (now Gorton) passing place and Rannoch Moor *c.* 1960. (J. L. Stevenson Collection)

the Highland Company's Pitlochry and Struan, as were the communities of Loch Rannoch and Strathtummel. But uppermost in Menzies's mind were his sporting lets, and he later attempted to restrict public use of the new road between Kinlochrannoch and Rannoch station, paid for by the West Highland Company, until the Perthshire local authorities intervened. That the West Highland was taken across Rannoch Moor appeased Breadalbane (above) and gratified Menzies. But the decision also turned on Sir John Stirling-Maxwell of Pollok, who purchased Corrour deer forest from Colonel Gustavus Walker of Lochtreighead in the expectation that he would be rail-served. The Corrour transaction required that Menzies and Cameron of Lochiel accept minor boundary changes by sale or excambion.[2] Walker had begun as an opponent but now acquiesced, which brought the line safely down Loch Treig into Brae Lochaber. Here, Lord Abinger and The MacKintosh held sway. The latter (initially a promoter but later disaffected) agreed to the Spean deviation, which usefully eliminated two of three viaducts, and the line continued to Fort William through Abinger's Inverlochy estate.[3] The Torlundy–Fort William deviation, which gave distiller MacDonald his sidings, also pleased Lady Abinger by taking the railway a little further from the windows of New Inverlochy Castle. (For deviations, see Appendix.)

Whatever the advantages and disadvantages of the Rannoch route, both cost and engineering difficulties had told against Forman's first survey (see Chapter 1). Rugged Glen Coe was not amenable to his economical 'contouring' technique and massive protection works could scarcely be avoided.4 The change of route lost the promoters support in Appin, Ballachulish, Onich and Ardgour, and meant that Lochiel's Nether Lochaber property was no longer directly served. (The loss of Roshven would leave his estate west of Fort William likewise untouched, save by the Banavie branch.) If privately disappointed, Lochiel nevertheless maintained that a railhead at Fort William satisfied his own needs, and he lost no opportunity to assert that the landed backers of the West Highland, in seeking the best route to the Arisaig coast, had made sacrifices for the public good. Lochiel would subsequently endorse the West Highland and Ballachulish extension, though insisting that his crofting tenants should not suffer unreasonable severance (see chapter 14).

That the Duke of Argyll volunteered his testimony was a major prize for the promoters. The Rosneath peninsula, he declared, could be served from West Highland Garelochhead, Lochfyneside from Arrochar & Tarbet.5 While North Argyll belonged to Callander & Oban and the Caledonian, the south of the county might look, with advantage, to the North British. This recalled the North British case in 1886/7, when that company backed the Clyde, Ardrishaig & Crinan Railway (see Chapter 1). Abinger and Lochiel did not recruit or attempt to over-persuade the proprietors who expressed doubts; it was sufficient that they refrained from opposition. Immediate set-backs were few. Sir John Ramsden of Ardverickie, while wishing the promoters well, warned that he would resist any future West Highland-to-Highland link by Loch Laggan. (Forman hinted, perhaps less than sincerely, at an alternative route by Glen Roy and the headwaters of the Spey.) The proposed deviation to firmer ground between Cruach and Corrour, on the highest reach of Rannoch Moor, was successfully resisted by the agents of the Appin (Downie) Trustees, as injuring their deer sanctuary in the Black Corries. By contrast, the Spean deviation, which invaded the club farms of The MacKintosh's crofter tenants, was approved with little debate. (For deviations, see Appendix.)

Factors and others

The estate factor was an important figure in rural Scotland. Fort William's Nigel MacKenzie, employed at one time or another by a clutch of western Highlands proprietors, is an outstanding example. George Malcolm, besides managing Glen Garry and Glen Quoich, was engaged by Stirling-Maxwell (above) to oversee Corrour. (Malcolm was also secretary of the Highland Landowners' Association.) James Wilson, The Colquhouns' factor, testified to the benefits expected along the Gare Loch and by Loch Long, while Breadalbane's William Dunn confirmed that the West Highland, as his master had conceded, met a public want. John Scott, factor for the Bullough family's Meggernie estate in Glen Lyon, organised the local petition-in-favour. He saw Bridge of Orchy as a railhead to supplement distant Aberfeldy (especially for sheep wintering) if the bridle path to Auch were made a metalled road, which did not happen. Ranald MacDonald, factor for the

Early days: Rannoch station, West Highland Railway: turntable-siding and improvised water tank on right. (J. Alsop collection)

Gordon-Cathcart estates in the Outer Hebrides, was a forceful advocate for Roshven; conversely, Alexander MacDonald of Portree, responsible for several Skye properties, argued from the first for Mallaig, which gained the day when Roshven was lost.

Witnesses of more than local standing included Fletcher Menzies (brother of William Menzies, above), who was secretary of the Highland Agricultural Society. He emphasised how house parties moved from place to place during the sporting season, generating rail traffic and benefitting the merchants who supplied the lodges. Duncan MacDiarmid of Camus Ericht (Loch Rannoch), a substantial cattle dealer, organised the district petition. His subsequent testimony was boldly imaginative: besides the traffic in domestic coal, general merchandise and livestock feedstuffs to be expected at Rannoch station, moorland peats might be sent to Fort William, fuelling MacDonald's distilleries and flavouring his whisky. Before the Lords Committee and again in the Commons, MacDiarmid unblushingly stated that Rannoch Moor saw relatively little snow and had a sure rock substratum. Though challenged by other witnesses, this went unchallenged by peers or MPs. Farmers whose support had been canvassed were occasionally 'obliged' with local use of the unfinished railway, and it appears that construction sidings remained available to Breadalbane's tenants at Auch and Achallader for some time after the West Highland opened. In March 1894 Lord Burton and his guests, en route to Glen Quoich lodge, were 'obliged' too, travelling all the way to Spean Bridge, over what was in several places still distinctly impermanent track. They had the use of contractor John Aird's saloon, changing to another vehicle at Rannoch; lunch was provided at Crianlarich.[6]

Conflicts

In May 1894, as the push to completion intensified, The MacKintosh threatened to interdict all work along the Spean deviation unless Inverlair was renamed Tulloch. The station stood on MacKintosh land, at the Treig-Spean confluence. Inverlair lodge lay across the river, in the Abinger estate. Broken promises were alleged and bad feeling may have arisen between The MacKintosh and the new Lord Abinger; but we may suspect that factor Allan MacDonald invented and maintained the quarrel in retaliation, after other differences with Formans & McCall. Inverlair, though not even a hamlet, was a known 'place', Tulloch just a tenant's farm – and there were 'Tullochs' elsewhere in the Highlands to confuse the traveller. MacKenzie could find nothing in the record, but saw no point in resisting. Lochiel agreed: he deprecated the behaviour of a fellow-proprietor, already amply compensated for his land, but thought it fatuous to battle over a signboard when The MacKintosh's goodwill would be needed if the proposed West Highland Kingussie Extension of 1893 were ever revived (see Chapter 14). From 1895 'Tulloch' was adopted.

Having offered facilities to Colonel Walker (above), the North British came to an agreement with Stirling-Maxwell, who planned an elaborate lodge and policies by Loch Ossian, served from Corrour.7 Passing place or private station, Corrour had at first an uncertain identity. The siding there lay unfinished for several months, and deliveries, including vulnerable saplings and hatchery trout, went astray. Stirling-Maxwell and his factor repeatedly clashed with North British officialdom, whose restrictive interpretation of working rules was upheld by general manager Conacher – perhaps because John Walker, his predecessor, had promised more than what was put in writing. There was useful traffic: construction materials necessarily came by train, and the contractor for the new lodge negotiated discounted fares to Glasgow, every pay-fortnight, for his workforce; in the longer run there would be coal and other supplies, and regular guests. To alienate Stirling-Maxwell – elected to Parliament in 1895 for a Glasgow constituency and ready to support the Mallaig Guarantee Bill – was by any test imprudent.

Behind Conacher's intransigence was anxiety that the Board of Trade would insist on expensive additions if Corrour's status were defined. To halt a passenger train needed prior clearance (often impractical) at Glasgow or Fort William, and the Corrour signalman risked reprimand if he acted without it. Before relaxing this cumbersome arrangement, Conacher demanded a list of accredited servants and visitors. He should consult a map, Stirling-Maxwell retorted – on these empty heights, what abuse could arise? For George Malcolm, 'next station charges' (reflecting Corrour's official non-existence) were the final provocation. Returning one evening to Invergarry, the factor refused to pay the Rannoch–Spean Bridge fare: purchasing a Tulloch–Spean Bridge ticket he proffered the Corrour–Tulloch excess and, when this was rejected, forwarded the same amount (in postage stamps) to district superintendent Arnott. An acrimonious correspondence ensued until the North British solicitor advised that

Corrour, West Highland Railway – from passing place to private, then public, station. (J. Alsop collection)

legal proceedings could not succeed. In the event, Corrour would graduate to public station (albeit a tiny one) without excessive outlay.[8]

Edward Place of Glen Dochart, his property an enclave within the vast Breadalbane lands, owned Crianlarich Hotel. He resisted the planned 'dining room' at West Highland Crianlarich and made difficulties over station access and water supply. Place found a lever in the protracted junction spur dispute, because the Board of Trade award required that he agree to sell a parcel of land (see Chapter 6). And it was an ominous complication when in 1894–5 Lord Breadalbane, whose influence could not be ignored, joined the newspaper campaign to have the spur opened without further delay. Reciting his own fractious dealings with the North British (and blaming Wieland rather than Conacher), he threatened to combine with the Fort William commissioners, the Loch Long 'residenters' and all other aggrieved parties along the West Highland. Government assistance for the Mallaig Extension should be absolutely conditional on the fulfilment of every earlier promise that the two companies had made. Conacher denied procrastination – Place's inflexibility was the explanation – but the record shows otherwise.

Chapter 10

Crisis

On the West Highland's opening day, Lord Tweeddale declared that the North British Company were now established in the western Highlands. Coexistence not expansion was though his underlying message. Though extension to Mallaig was essential, though a connection with the Highland Railway in Strathspey or a branch to Ballachulish would be considered, the time had come for the Caledonian Company, the Highland and the North British to respect one another's territory. The Great Glen Agreement of 1889, Tweeddale implied, would remain in being (which ruled out a West Highland advance on Inverness until 1904). As for relations with the Callander & Oban, he relied on but did not specify the Peace Agreement (properly, New Lines Agreement) of 1891. This required Caledonian and North British to define the districts that each claimed exclusively, with other districts shared. Previous treaties of the kind had broken down, but this time there was robust provision for arbitration by high court judge Lord Watson. Both companies were chastened by their expensive and inconclusive contest, during two parliamentary sessions (1889–91), to possess the Glasgow & South Western Railway. It had been the barren culmination of a barren twenty years' warfare. Both now wanted to limit the territorial disputes that gave opportunities to outside promoters. John Conacher, briefed to seek co-existence with the Caledonian, had succeeded pugnacious John Walker. He regarded the West Highland as a dubious burden which the contributory traffic of the Mallaig Extension would eventually relieve.

In hindsight, the New Lines Agreement was indeed a turning point. On to 1914, Caledonian and North British would maintain a grudging détente. In 1894, however, peace seemed far from certain. John Anderson of the Callander & Oban, for the moment unchecked by the Caledonian, was ready for a fresh thrust into Lochaber. Moreover, the Highland–North British treaty had been endangered during 1893, when Charles Forman made a survey through the Great Glen, seeking financial support for an independent promotion. He was his own master, unwilling to be constrained. Thus, North British haste to see the West Highland open had not been the only irritant when Conacher clashed with Charles Forman. A halfway Great Glen project (i.e. from the West Highland in Glen Spean to Fort Augustus) would be sufficient, Forman had suggested, to nullify the Ten Years Truce, setting Highland and North British at loggerheads, whereupon his backers need only wait on events to recoup their investment: one company or the other would take up the scheme... Forman had on hand, too, the Glasgow Central Railway (opened in 1896), which strengthened the Caledonian's position on the north bank of the lower Clyde. It was in part to head off this threat that the North British had supported the West Highland in the first place.[1]

Lord Burton, George Malcolm and other Great Glen activists disliked the 1889 Agreement, but they had not been ready to denounce it. Though at odds when the West Highland Mallaig Extension Bill went to Parliament, Conacher and Andrew Dougall, secretary-manager of the Highland Railway, were alike relieved when the rumoured Great Glen bill did not materialise (see Chapters 11 and 12). Forman's venture had faded away. But his reputation as a fluent salesman adept in exploiting inter-company tensions was reinforced. An Inverness businessman afterwards described him as a 'tug boat with a string of barges' – i.e. unwary investors.

Moreover, these machinations had perturbed the Highland board, who remembered that in 1888/9 they, like their Caledonian counterparts, came to understand too late how far the West Highland project had matured. Unconvinced of North British good faith and fearful of a new threat to Inverness, within weeks of the West Highland's opening the Highland Company chose pre-emptive occupation of the Great Glen and announced their Spean Bridge & Fort William Extension, surveyed by their own engineer, Murdoch Paterson. The North British at once endorsed a rival scheme, the West Highland Inverness Extension, for which Forman's plans of the previous year were hastily purchased. There was no deep-laid plot, and the Highland directors had been overly nervous.

The railway press hailed the impending contest with excitement. The Mallaig Extension, though controversial, was less newsworthy. For neutral spectators the debate over subsidy was tiresomely ideological and common sense suggested that the West Highland route, whether a paying proposition or not, should be completed to the coast as first intended. By contrast an old-fashioned railway war, in the unlikely setting of the Great Glen, provided excellent copy. It was all the better when the Callander& Oban Company joined in, lodging their Ballachulish, Fort William & Banavie Extension Bill – which promised, in conjunction with the Highland project, a direct Oban-Inverness link quite independent of the West Highland. Talk of a latter-day railway mania scarcely seemed exaggerated when Fort William (with fewer than 2,000 inhabitants) might soon have *three* stations – West Highland at the pierhead; Highland down the Linnhe shore (with its own pier and reached by an expensive tunnel) and Callander & Oban on the hillside.

The Highland scheme was primarily an Inverness–Spean Bridge line for through running to and from the south. It approached West Highland Spean Bridge from Gairlochy, along the River Spean. Its Fort William arm kept to the Great Glen, following the River Lochy (as the Glasgow & North Western would have done), and

Gairlochy station, Invergarry & Fort Augustus Railway *c.* 1930. Here Glen Spean debouches into the Great Glen. (Courtesy of D. Yuill)

this included a spur to Banavie, diverging near Torcastle. Forman's proposed Great Glen line, taken up by the North British on behalf of the West Highland, began from a junction west of Roy Bridge, climbing behind Tirindrish and dropping to Loch Lochy past Invergloy. For through running between Fort William and Inverness he added a 2-mile spur from Auchindaul, crossing the Spean at High Bridge. Murdoch's line would have crossed at the same point, turning east to Spean Bridge. Ignoring North British displeasure, Forman laid out the Callander & Oban branch. With Fort William's seafront now occupied by the West Highland, while the Highland planned their tunnel (above), he found a higher alignment behind the town.[2] The coastal route from Connel Ferry entailed three sea-loch viaducts, across Loch Etive, Loch Creran and Loch Leven, to be designed by Sir John Wolfe-Barry, of Tower Bridge fame.

The Callander & Oban scheme duplicated the West Highland Banavie branch, which was still under construction. This, though clearly unnecessary, underscored the Caledonian Company's mischief-making case that, west from Banavie, the Mallaig Extension (now authorised but awaiting a firm pledge of government assistance) might be jointly operated. A line subsidised by the state must belong to all-comers, and traffic should be cultivated by every possible connecting route, maximising revenue and reducing the taxpayer's obligation. The Callander & Oban Bill specified joint ownership of the Mallaig Extension 'to secure to the public the fullest use of [an] undertaking [aided] by public funds.' Having likewise provided for a Banavie link (above), the Highland Company would be able to present the same claim. Though Tweeddale obtained the Treasury's assurance that joint arrangements would not be entertained, North British anxieties persisted. Another version of the ominous Caledonian argument lurked behind the unresolved question of exchange at Crianlarich (see Chapter 6). What if the Caledonian were to bid for Crianlarich–Fort William running powers over the West Highland, so as to access the Mallaig line?

The magisterial *Financial Times* judged that the North British had themselves to blame: they were invaders, who had not guaranteed the West Highland 'for... the West Highland's own sweet self'. Retaliation was inevitable:

> [The] Caledonian and Highland Directors ... do not mean to lie down and quietly submit to aggression.

And the North British, locked in to their West Highland 'folly', could not rest content at Fort William, a 'nowhere in particular' terminus. For worthwhile through traffic, they must aim at Inverness. It all spelt a protracted contest.

But the *Dundee Advertiser*, in jocular mood, caught the bubble quality of these promotions:

> It was an old Roman boast that all roads lead to Rome. Very soon a Lochaber man will be able to boast that all railways lead to Fort William. The town that ... had no railway at all will ... have one from the east, one from the south, one from the west, and one from the north. Why, the metropolis of 'Long John' will become another Perth or Carlisle and Cockney tourists in great numbers will sample the local manufacture at the station as they wait for trains.[3]

Signs increased that the rival Great Glen schemes were after all evanescent. The North British were represented on the Highland Railway board by virtue of their shared interests at Perth. Tweeddale, in this capacity, made overtures to the Highland chairman, Aeneas MacKintosh of Raigmore. By February of 1895 both companies had decided on the face-saving formula that other commitments precluded a costly and not yet urgent Great Glen line. Both bills were withdrawn. The 1889 Agreement was restored, in modified form – neither Highland nor North British were to countenance any halfway project, at either end of the Glen. Meanwhile, to combat the Connel Ferry–Banavie scheme, the North British had invoked the New Lines Agreement. Pending arbitration, Caledonian general manager James Thompson refused to rein in the Callander & Oban. (He was ready to argue that the Arisaig seaboard and Skye, by virtue of steamer routes touching Oban, must remain a shared district, if and when the West Highland Mallaig Extension was built.) But the arbiter ruled in favour of the North British, and, under Caledonian pressure, the Callander & Oban abandoned their bill.

All in all the North British endured a tense few months.[4] In the event, the Great Glen was 'locked up' once more and the Caledonian conceded that a Callander & Oban and West Highland boundary might be drawn at Loch Leven. Though Caledonian and Highland would continue to oppose government aid for the Mallaig Extension, there was now little fear of their changing tack to demand running powers or joint ownership. *That* suggestion had been calculated to delay and obstruct. While happy to turn the tables, putting the West Highland intruder on the defensive, and in no mood to accommodate the West Highland's patron, Caledonian and Highland were concerned above all for their own territorial interests. They recognised, though resentfully, that the North British were similarly minded and not bent on further aggression.

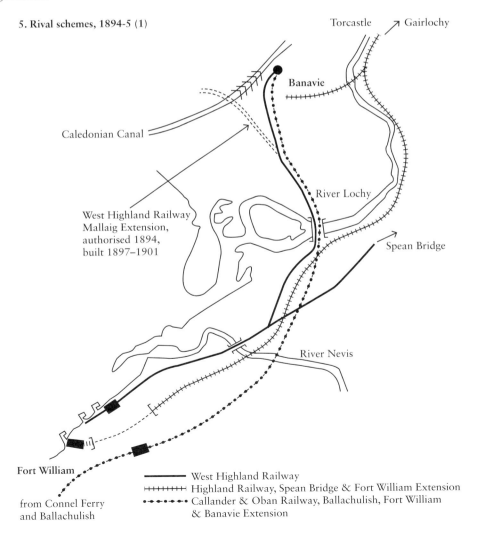

5. Rival schemes, 1894-5 (1)

Torcastle
Gairlochy
Banavie
Caledonian Canal
River Lochy
West Highland Railway
Mallaig Extension,
authorised 1894,
built 1897–1901
Spean Bridge
River Nevis
Fort William

from Connel Ferry
and Ballachulish

—————— West Highland Railway
++++++++ Highland Railway, Spean Bridge & Fort William Extension
•••••••• Callander & Oban Railway, Ballachulish, Fort William
& Banavie Extension

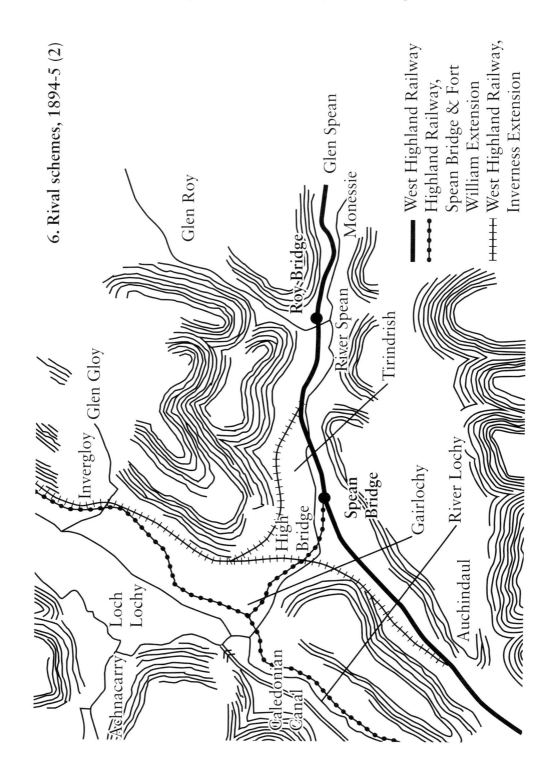

6. Rival schemes, 1894-5 (2)

West Highland Railway

Highland Railway,
Spean Bridge & Fort
William Extension

West Highland Railway,
Inverness Extension

Glen Spean

Glen Roy

Roy Bridge

Monessie

River Spean

Tirindrish

Invergloy

Glen Gloy

High
Bridge

Spean
Bridge

Gairlochy

River Lochy

Loch
Lochy

Auchindaul

Achnacarry

Caledonian
Canal

Chapter 11

The Mallaig Extension

The Roshven landowner, Professor Hugh Blackburn, opposed a Fort William–Loch Ailort line, as did the Earl of Morton, whose Conaglen estate included an outlying lodge at Craigag. In 1888/9, both proprietors resisted the blandishments of Abinger and Cameron of Lochiel, and Blackburn tellingly challenged the design of the proposed harbour. They were blamed, conveniently but over-simply, when the West Highland's Roshven arm was lost. The North British commitment to *any* extension west of Banavie was, despite fair words, essentially 'wait and see'. Without assistance in some form, the West Highland promoters lacked the means to continue their line

To the ROYAL COMMISSION on the WESTERN HIGHLANDS and ISLANDS, this Petition of Residents on the Western Islands and adjacent Mainland, Humbly Sheweth:—

I. That the herring fishery in Lochs Nevis, Hourn, Slapin, Eishort, and others, and in the Sound of Sleat, the Little Minch, near Barra, and elsewhere, is very large and important; and that there are many rich fishing-banks, capable of employing profitably a large number of people in winter fishing, off this coast and the adjacent islands.

II. That this is a pastoral district; and that, under the present system of Sheep-farming, it is necessary to winter away a considerable portion of the sheep stock.

III. That your petitioners are gravely hampered in the profitable prosecution of sheep-farming and fishing, their staple industries, by the want of means of quick communication with Southern markets and wintering grounds.

IV. That the construction of a Railway terminating at Mallaig would largely obviate the disadvantages under which your petitioners labour.

V. That Mallaig lies, practically, on the course of vessels passing North and South along this coast. That it could be easily made an excellent harbour, and that it is the best point on the West Coast for the Terminus of a Railway to serve the Islands North of Coll, and South of Lochmaddy, and the Mainland opposite.

VI. That, to the Islands of Canna, Rum, and Muke, there is at present no regular post; and to Eigg a post only once a week; and that these, and other islands as far West as Barra, which is 60 knots West of Mallaig, might easily have a daily post by steamer from Mallaig on the completion of a Railway to that point, and that postal arrangements on the mainland could be similarly improved.

VII. That the proposed Railway would not be a "competing line," but would serve a large district which is at present entirely destitute of Railway accommodation, as Mallaig is about 70 and 40 miles distant respectively from Oban and Strome Ferry, the nearest existing Railway Stations, and 50 miles from Fort-William.

VIII. That the construction of light Railways across Skye, to some point on its East Coast, nearly opposite Mallaig, would be of great value to the inhabitants of Skye and the Long Island.

Your petitioners, therefore, beg that your Commission will favourably consider their suggestions, and make such recommendations as may ensure the construction of a Railway to Mallaig, and of light Railways in Skye.

And your Petitioners will ever pray.

Model competition in favour of 'Loch Eil & Mallaig Railway', Lothian Commission, 1889/90.

beyond Lochaber; and the House of Lords Committee declined to award powers which could only lie in abeyance. In the short run the objections of Morton and Blackburn could be down-played, leaving the promoters to boast how no proprietor in the 100 miles between Craigendoran and Fort William had dissented. In the longer run the West Highland Company, having met the Napier Commission's prescription (a private-enterprise line into Lochaber), would be strong contenders for government aid, whenever the Roshven project, or some equivalent, could be revived.

Quoting the measures taken to improve transport in Ireland, by way of antidote to Home Rule sentiment, the rising Liberal Unionist politician Joseph Chamberlain wanted 'equal treatment' for the Highlands and Islands. A convert to national efficiency (and, specifically, to the expansion of Scotland's west coast fishery, reducing Britain's food imports), Chamberlain favoured the creation of additional rail-served harbours. Lochiel foresaw that Lord Salisbury's Conservative Government, which enjoyed Liberal Unionist support, would be obliged to declare their intentions before the West Highland was completed to Fort William. And so it proved. The Lothian Commission, which reported in 1890, and the ensuing Treasury Committee (1890/1) came down in favour of two schemes, one south and one north of the Dingwall & Skye Railway. 'North of Strome', four projects were in contention – the Garve & Ullapool Railway, authorised in 1890; Achnasheen–Aultbea (like the Ullapool line, diverging from the Dingwall & Skye); Culrain–Lochinver and Invershin–Loch Laxford (these last making junction with the Far North line to Wick and Thurso). The Highland Company offered to work, maintain and partially finance a Lochinver railway, whether built from Garve via Ullapool or cross-country from Culrain, provided that Mallaig was ruled out, but the Treasury sternly declined to bargain.

'South of Strome', an extension of the West Highland was the obvious option, with Roshven superseded by Mallaig, at the mouth of Loch Nevis, as terminus-cum-harbour. Influential voices in Skye outweighed opinion in the middle islands of the Outer Hebrides, whence Roshven offered a shorter passage. More than the Highland's hostility, North British ambivalence kept the Mallaig project in doubt, and the Garve & Ullapool promoters, with the (qualified) endorsement of the Highland Company, had already won their Act.[1] The landlords friendly to the West Highland feared that, without a fresh initiative, government assistance would be forfeit, and John Baird of Knoydart commissioned a new survey. Engineer Alexander Simpson, of Simpson & Wilson, costed the 40-mile route from Banavie by Glenfinnan and Arisaig to Mallaig, retracing Charles Forman's line as far as Kinlochailort.[2] The resulting Loch Eil & Mallaig Railway was submitted to the Lothian Commission as a landowners' scheme on which the North British could be expected to look favourably. During 1891/2, Cameron of Lochiel helped bring together the ostensible promoters, the North British, the Treasury and the Scottish Office. With a Conservative offer of subsidy on the table from June 1892, Baird's scheme could go forward – now generally known as the Mallaig Extension. Procedural quirks (seized on by the Caledonian Company and the Highland) prevented a late bill in parliamentary session 1892/3, and

Alexander Simpson. (Courtesy of J. Shipway)

authorisation required another parliamentary round in 1893/4. The West Highland Railway Mallaig Extension Act would receive the royal assent just in time for the West Highland's opening to Fort William.

From George Wieland, the North British-cum-West Highland secretary, Baird obtained the terms of a working and maintenance agreement. His proprietors' alliance, echoing the coalition that had helped the West Highland Bill through Parliament in 1889, included Professor Blackburn (above) and Colonel John MacDonald of Glenaladale (Loch Shiel), a veteran of the Roshven campaign. Lochiel, as a West Highland director, was at first the go-between but took the lead when Baird fell ill. That the North British shaped events is more than likely – the company had ties with the Baird family at large, who were North Lanarkshire ironmasters. General manager Walker had temporised after 1889, but under Conacher a clear policy emerged. The North British would rewrite their West Highland guarantee and working agreement to embrace the entire route from Craigendoran to Mallaig, provided that subsidy was first of all in place. They would entrust the line to Simpson & Wilson, deemed safer (i.e. more biddable) than Formans & McCall.3 Lochiel had always argued that the West Highland would become profitable by reaching the coast. Conacher and chairman Tweeddale were unconvinced, but they recognised that a finite additional outlay, securing a sizeable contributory traffic for the West Highland proper, was the best bargain for North British shareholders.

The Conservatives had come to believe that economic stimulus could combat distress and unrest in 'backward' regions of the British Isles. The Liberals, more inclined to fundamental land reform, saw government subsidy as a palliative – and one from which vested interests (i.e. landowners and railway companies) stood to gain. The political Left held that the Caledonian Railway and the North British possessed ample means to sustain new lines, even loss-making ones – though the Highland Company, existing within narrow margins, perhaps deserved benefit of doubt. In any case, if the North British had miscalculated in backing the West Highland, why should the taxpayer remedy their error? In the circumstances it was prudential to maintain, thin though the pretence had become, that the West Highland and now the West Highland Extension were in origin 'landowners' lines'. After the Salisbury Government had acceded to Lochiel's formula (a grant for Mallaig harbour and a Treasury guarantee on a large part of the railway's capital), the minority Liberal Government of 1892–5 were reluctant to confirm it, despite the opinion of civil servants that they must. Sir William Harcourt, Chancellor of the Exchequer, was personally opposed. Only in 1894, after traffic on the West Highland had begun, did he undertake (prodded on all sides) to bring in the necessary bill.

Ireland dominated the Liberals' agenda. Sustained by the Irish Nationalists, the aged prime minister, William Gladstone, attempted, unsuccessfully, to carry Home Rule. Thereafter, his party drifted to resignation under Lord Roseberry, when Salisbury resumed office. The General Election of 1895 saw Conservatives and Liberal dissidents (Chamberlain included) combine in a victorious Unionist alliance, but still the Mallaig Guarantee hung fire. If designated a consensual measure, Harcourt's bill might have continued that session, but the Opposition parties would not cooperate, which obliged the Treasury to begin again. James Dalziel, heading the unreconciled Liberals, was MP for Kirkcaldy; he condemned the North British Company's monopoly of Fife, where their misconduct and broken promises had disqualified them, he asserted, from state assistance for *any* purpose. Irish Nationalist resistance was resented in Scotland – they were denying the Scottish Highlands aid which Ireland had already received. With Inverness-shire's Unionists pledged to the Mallaig project, James Baillie was returned, though himself equivocal (see Chapter 3), and the Liberals muttered that Lochiel and other landlords had wielded improper influence.[4]

Closely fought to the end, the Guarantee Bill of 1895/6 faced wrecking amendments. Sir William Hicks-Beach, Harcourt's Unionist successor, resisted calls for a Treasury presence on the West Highland board. He conceded annual inspection by the Board of Trade for the duration of the Guarantee, which the North British could not refuse.[5] Half the *gross* income of the Mallaig Extension was reserved, offsetting the Treasury's contribution. That the remainder would meet operating costs was questionable, and the North British, in agreeing to work the line at 50 per cent, were likely to incur an added burden. They proposed a division of *net* earnings after local authority rates and miscellaneous charges had been deducted. Hicks-Beach refused, but he allowed that the railway west from Banavie would be valued for rates as if unimproved land. Last-ditch opponents turned to the Light Railways Bill (Act of 1896), which paralleled the Guarantee Bill through Parliament. They urged a complete re-examination of the Mallaig scheme, which should receive no greater assistance than an equivalent light line might obtain. With the Guarantee Act at last in place, the Mallaig contract was awarded to Robert McAlpine.

Chapter 12

Great Glen

In Lochaber and along the Great Glen, the Glasgow & North Western Railway of 1882/3 had raised hopes only to disappoint. Solicitor Charles Innes of Innes & MacKay, Inverness, became the promoters' agent, along with Nigel MacKenzie in Fort William. Sir Arthur Bass, with a long lease of Glen Quoich, was thoroughly committed: the brewer MP, newly a baronet, would become Lord Burton (1886). Lord Abinger and Cameron of Lochiel, whose lands marched at the River Lochy, were ready to engage. Factor George Malcolm met with engineer Walrond-Smith during his survey. However, the Ellice family, who owned Glen Garry and Glen Quoich, were averse to an obtrusive line along Loch Oich, and Lord Lovat at Fort Augustus was hostile. The proprietors on either side of Loch Ness remained loyal to the Highland Railway. In sum, landlord hostility doomed the Glasgow & North Western. At least 60 miles of route between Glasgow and Fort William met with objection, where the Duke of Montrose and the Marquess of Breadalbane made formidable opponents. The North British dithered (see Chapter 1). It was altogether a lesson for Abinger and Lochiel. They would take care when, half a dozen years later, the West Highland was promoted that the North British were engaged beforehand and that no landowner between Craigendoran and Fort William stayed an active enemy.

Charles Forman's Great Glen scheme of 1893 had dwindled away, but by 1895 a different situation obtained. The Great Glen Agreement had collapsed, only to be restored (see Chapter 10). The Highland Company's promotion, it was generally believed, had been designed only to block the way to Inverness – if granted powers to build, they would have delayed indefinitely. But the West Highland Inverness Extension was taken seriously, not least by Innes, who had campaigned energetically (encouraged by the North British), influencing opinion throughout the Glen.[1] Abandonment cost the West Highland much good will. Malcolm was already critical of North British half-heartedness (as he saw it) in developing the West Highland's traffic, and he grew increasingly disgruntled too by his experience as factor at Corrour (see Chapter 9).

The repaired Agreement was no more proof against independent ventures than the original. Highland and North British had covenanted not to countenance any

ames and Rents of the different Shootings (including Deer Forests)
within the District which might be served by the Proposed Line,
as shown on the Plan coloured Pink.

PARISH.	NAME OF SHOOTING.	RENT.			TOTAL.		
oleskine	Knockie	£315	0	0			
	Cullochy	530	0	0			
	Glendoe	630	0	0			
	Dell	300	0	0			
	Corriegarth and Killin ...	1,010	0	0			
	Stronelairg	361	0	0			
	Garrogy	320	0	0			
	Foyers	150	0	0			
	Inchnacardoch...	1,190	0	0			
	Aberchalder	170	0	9			
	Ardochy	235	0	0	£5,211	0	0
Urquhart	Kilmartin	£230	0	0			
	Corriemony	720	0	0			
	Balmacaan	3,045	0	0			
	Invermoriston	790	0	0			
	Dundreggan and Ceanacroc ...	1,815	0	0			
	North Ceanacroc (Lord Tweed-						
	mouth)	2,500	0	0	8,100	0	0
Kilmonivaig	Invergarry	£1,500	0	0			
	Glenquoich	3,110	0	0			
	Aberchalder	549	0	0			
	Glenfintaig	337	0	0			
	Altrua	105	0	0			
	Invergloy	250	0	0			
	Corriegour	140	0	0	5,991	0	0
Kilmallie	Achnacarry	£1,500	0	0			
	Glenkingie and Glendessary...	1,200	0	0			
	Inverskillivulin	140	0	0	2,840	0	0
	Total ...				£22,142	0	0

Invergarry & Fort Augustus Railway Bill, 1895/6, evidence of sporting estate traffic. (Author's collection)

halfway promotion, but the Invergarry & Fort Augustus Railway was just that, echoing Forman's scheme three years earlier. Malcolm rallied local support. With Lord Burton as leading promoter, a bill was lodged for parliamentary session 1895/6. In defiance of Highland and North British efforts to preserve a no man's land, the

Great Glen south from Fort Augustus would be linked to the West Highland at Spean Bridge. Forman laid out the 20-mile route: it dropped by High Bridge, climbed into Glen Gloy and descended again along Loch Lochy to the valley floor; by the south-eastern shore of Loch Oich, opposite Invergarry, it continued to Aberchalder and Fort Augustus. A short but expensive extension, spanning both the Caledonian Canal and the River Oich, led to a new pier on Loch Ness.[2] Geography prescribed a facing junction in the down direction at Spean Bridge, which meant reversal for Fort William–Fort Augustus trains. Local traffic did not justify a supplementary spur, and exchange at Spean Bridge might suffice for passenger business. The promoters cultivated an 'all above board' tone. Their resources were adequate. Their line, which would serve half a dozen sporting estates at the same time as benefitting the whole population, could not hinder the later, larger scheme into which it might eventually be absorbed. No doubt new projects for a railway all along the Great Glen would re-emerge, but that was not their concern.

This was disingenuous. The promotion, though solidly supported locally, was also speculative. This time the Great Glen Truce must be destroyed beyond repair, when, with Highland and North British once more embroiled, the investors could expect to sell out advantageously. The Invergarry & Fort Augustus was in this respect a 'contractor's line', talked up by Forman and by Glasgow solicitors Keyden, Strang &

Spean Bridge station, West Highland Railway. Alterations to accomodate the Invergarry & Augustus Railway included a conventional signal box. (J. L. Stevenson collection)

Spean Bridge Junction, West Highland Railway/Invergarry & Fort Augustus Railway. The original elaborate layout spoke of ambitions to reach Inverness. (J. L. Stevenson Collection)

Girvan, who became the agents (Innes & MacKay were found a subordinate role).[3] But, fragile though it had proved, the Great Glen Agreement, like the more durable New Lines Agreement between Caledonian and North British, signalled changing times. Rising costs and legislative restrictions on railway companies' freedom of action inclined them towards co-existence, and they could resist manipulation more confidently. Outside ventures were more likely to stall or be thrown back on their own resources – ultimately the forlorn fate of the Invergarry & Fort Augustus Company who won their Act in 1896 in the face of determined Highland and North British resistance.

The principal promoters and would-be directors (besides Burton) were Sir Donald Matheson of Dalquhurn, the leading Turkey Red dyer in the Vale of Leven; John Neilson, a prominent Glasgow ironmaster; J. C. Cunninghame of Craigends, Renfrewshire; and Emmanuel Ristori, engineer-director of North British Aluminium. Only Ristori, whose company established a pioneering smelter at Foyers (Loch Ness), and Cunnighame, with a property at Upper Foyers, could claim direct involvement with the district.[4] Speculative interest, not prior intimacy, united them. In order that Burton and his allies might 'know a little more of each other', a dinner was organised in January 1896 at a London club. Forman and Malcolm both attended; the latter, acting more and more for Burton, would eventually join the Invergarry & Fort Augustus board. Other moneyed sportsmen applauded, like the Duke of Portland, who leased the Oich and Garry fishings, but a showing by Great Glen proprietors was indispensable. The Invergarry Trustees were recruited in the person of Captain Edward Ellis (whose doubts persisted). The new Lord Abinger lent his name but was often absent from Lochaber. Lochiel, whose crofters, like Abinger's, would gain a station at Gairlochy, declared neutrality. He was a West Highland director, bound by the Great Glen Agreement. Lovat could not be won over.

Highland and North British, though mutually suspicious, mounted a common opposition. Parliament, they argued, had tacitly endorsed their Great Glen treaty as an adjunct of the West Highland Act in 1889. Both companies protested that a Great Glen line in any form was not yet needed, but counsel for the Invergarry & Fort Augustus Bill condemned their 'inaction':

> They neither of them care that the other should make [a railway], they neither of them want to make it at present; they want to lock up the country in order that they may quarrel from time to time as to who is to make [it].

Forman submitted that the Invergarry & Fort Augustus was a bona fide, practical scheme. Traffic on the southern half of the Caledonian Canal would be captured; on the northern half of the waterway (i.e. on Loch Ness) the promoters would support an improved steamer service.[5] Thus the entire Glen would be better served, pending the eventual completion of an end-to-end line, to which Highland and North British, if taken at their word, remained committed. In the meantime the Highland could have nothing to fear, and a branch, boosting West Highland income would be presented to the North British. In the breathing space thus afforded, the two companies might hammer out a compromise whereby the through rail route could be completed. When a line to Inverness became reality, the North British could restore, if they chose, the cut-off from Roy Bridge and the High Bridge spur proposed in 1894/5.

The Highland Company's long-serving Andrew Dougall had departed as something of a scapegoat after it was revealed that the company's accounting practice during his tenure had exaggerated their solvency. Charles Steel, their new general manager, attempted to turn this embarrassment to advantage. The Highland must avoid unnecessary burdens. If they were driven to costly measures in defence of Inverness, other desirable schemes would be dropped or delayed. Conacher, for the North British, cited the West Highland's 'disappointing' earnings. A feeder to Spean Bridge could make little difference in the short run, and assistance for a premature project was out of the question. Malcolm, he claimed, had angled for a quite unrealistic North British guarantee. Conacher conceded that the Highland Company had long since earned a say in how and when a Great Glen line should be achieved. He wanted the same say for North British shareholders, burdened by the West Highland, who would have to supplement such government aid as the West Highland Extension might obtain. The North British, moreover, claimed ownership of Forman's earlier surveys, purchased in 1894 (see Chapter 10). The Invergarry & Fort Augustus promoters, Conacher concluded, sought to foist their project on the North British, and they all expected to profit – 'to go out with something', engineer and agents too. Steel, equally blunt, castigated 'Mr Forman's tendency to project lines'. The promoters hoped to 'force the hands of [others], to make this line or to take it over'. Their asking price would reflect the strategic value of the powers which Parliament might grant them, not their modest potential traffic.

Both managers insisted that postponement was the rational course. A stopgap halfway line was a needless complication, sure to provoke more conflict. It was indeed Lochiel's great fear during 1896 that warfare in the Great Glen would resume, distracting the North British from the delicate negotiations that finally settled the Mallaig line's Treasury Guarantee. Across Lochaber feeling was divided, as it had been in 1894/5. Fort William as a fledgling railway town might be disadvantaged if bypassed by Glasgow–Great Glen trains (cf. the Glasgow & North Western, with the burgh on its intended route). An easterly link by Loch Laggan into Strathspey might be more valuable than a Great Glen line that went no further than Fort Augustus. The former would bring local traffic to Fort William, but the latter offered connection cross-country both with the Highland Railway (though circuitously in respect of Inverness and the Far North) and with the Great North of Scotland.

Burton, Malcolm and Innes escaped the taint of speculation. There was genuine local enthusiasm – to be seen not least in the campaigning partnership of Leo Linse, Lord Abbot of the Benedictine foundation at Fort Augustus, and his Free Church colleague, Reverend John MacKay. But the promoters were guided (like their little company afterwards) from outside by their main agents, who might more wisely have deferred to Innes. An ill-informed attempt to recruit MacKenzie ended farcically – *his* brief, on behalf of the West Highland, was to *discredit* the Invergarry & Fort Augustus. This he undertook with characteristic gusto, staging bogus local meetings, which duplicated genuine, well-attended occasions, then planting press reports of empty halls and an indifferent public. Despite their heady victory in 1896, an air of unreality clung to the enterprise, as illustrated by the reluctance of Lord Burton (who spent only part of each year at Glen Quoich) to forego his deer stalking for urgent railway matters.

Chapter 13

Progress, 1895–6

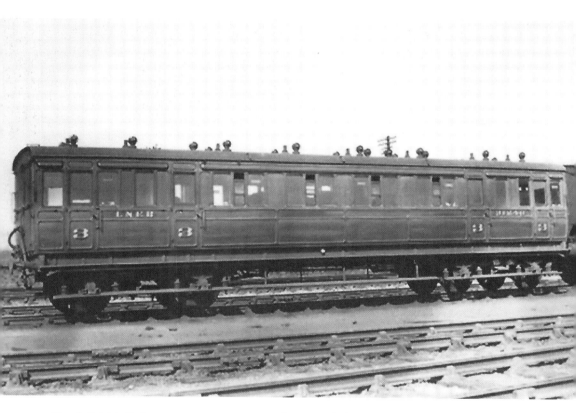

North British Railway compartment-cum-saloon coach for West Highland Railway service, 1894 (in altered condition *c.* 1925). (Courtesy of R. W. Lynn)

The bogie coaches designed by Matthew Holmes for the West Highland Railway – compartment-cum-saloon, with an eye to tourist traffic – were far superior to North British passenger rolling stock in general, and comparison did not flatter the Highland Company's spartan vehicles. Similar coaches, a little altered, were allocated to summer workings between Edinburgh and Fort William from 1895. Trains were strengthened with six-wheel North British coaches, and the East Coast stock for London–Fort William service was likewise of this traditional pattern. (Elderly rigid wheelbase vehicles would make up the Banavie locals.) The seemingly lavish provision of new-built locomotives drew favourable comment – a misapprehension in that Holmes's 'West Highland bogie' 4-4-0s struggled uphill with any load heavier than standard, which meant much double-heading. Their air-brake reservoirs were inadequate and the long descents required repeated application of the manual (screw-operated) tender brake. Fort William's 4-4-0s were rostered to allow frequent replacement of their tender brake-blocks at Cowlairs.

Summer business was immediately buoyant. Eventually 'Mallaig fish', and the corresponding empties, would need timetabled paths. Traffic superintendent Deuchars wanted shorter headways; he proposed splitting at least a few of the sections north from Garelochhead. The signal cabins might be switched in and out – Highland and Callander & Oban had adopted this solution to peaks and troughs of traffic. At some locations additional passing loops were desirable too.

New signal box/loop	Dividing
Whistlefield/Finnart	Garelochhead–Glen Douglas
Inveruglas	Arrochar & Tarbet–Ardlui
Glen Falloch	Ardlui–Crianlarich
Auch	Tyndrum–Bridge of Orchy
Achallader	Bridge of Orchy–Gortan
Cainib	Rannoch–Corrour
Lochtreighead	Corrour–Tulloch
Auchindaul	Spean Bridge–Banavie Junction

Conacher preferred to tolerate double-heading. The water columns at Garelochhead, Ardlui, Crianlarich, Bridge of Orchy and Tulloch might be duplicated to minimise delays. This programme, though only partially completed, helped set the enduring West Highland pattern of infrequent, often lengthy, trains. Until the end of steam, summer brought impressive Crianlarich 'meets' when two heavy services crossed and all four engines took water.

The West Highland, once opened, escaped serious accident until the autumn of 1895.[1] On a dark and blustery October evening, having missed Shandon's distant signal, the driver of the leading engine on an up service came abruptly into the station on the down road, as the signalman rushed to reset the points. The train divided and one coach was dragged at right angles over the island platform, badly injuring a female passenger. Major Marindin, as investigating officer, concluded that neither of Shandon's distants had been lit and found the signalman negligent, which partly excused the driver who had been working a long shift, Glasgow–Fort William and return.[2] Marindin took the opportunity to reiterate his misgivings, expressed in 1894, that at intermediate stations on the West Highland the tablet instruments were secured in the stationmaster's office and not in the signal cabin, though this was not a directly contributory factor. The interlocking he considered faulty:

> Had the points ... been activated by the same lever as the locking bar the signalman could not have moved them and the whole train would have run [safely] into the station on the wrong line.

In May of 1896, a down morning passenger was derailed, with no harm beyond jolting and bruises, almost at journey's end, where the Torlundy curves gave way to the long straight towards Banavie Junction. After ballast and up passenger passed safely, the blazing early summer sun had distorted the track. At this spot, claimed the enginemen, the permanent way was suspect, while the engineer's inspector alleged excessive speeds, but no one was held to blame.

Though centre of a wide district, Fort William was a small town with housing in short supply. North British railwaymen, obliged to make-shift, competed for the 'temporary booking office' (a superior wooden hut), which became available when Lucas & Aird completed the passenger station. Signalman William Holden occupied 'the west end of the temporary goods office', bequeathed, some months later, to driver Alexander Williamson. Signal and telegraph inspector William Aitchison took lonely lodgings, while his wife and children stayed behind in far-away Montrose. His own store-cum-office was eventually partitioned to provide a home of sorts. It was suggested that Aitchison be excused payment, but general manager Conacher demurred: 'Other servants in temporary accommodation are paying rent'. He permitted only a 3d reduction, from 1s 6d to 1s 3d weekly. After a cheerless winter the refurbished barracks at the old fort, first converted to dwellings forty years earlier and now the West Highland Company's property, came to seem relatively attractive. On the waiting list at May term, besides Aitchison, Holden and Williamson, were stationmaster James Blackwood, drivers James Kay and Robert Beattie, and platelayers Christopher MacDonald and Alexander MacKay. Already resident were surfaceman Norman Ross and fencer Donald Nicolson, earlier employed by Lucas & Aird. Citing his length of service, Beattie appealed to Holmes for priority over the engineer's recent recruits, who 'did not intend to bring their wives'.

Blackwood declined the let offered on the grounds that the fort was 'nearly two hundred years old and...not a desirable place of abode'. It went instead to William Clarkson, the regular driver of the Fort William ballast. District superintendent Arnott was unsympathetic; the house reserved for Blackwood had been 'much better than the others':

> His objections are merely sentimental [and] he should be told either to take it or we will cease paying his expenses.

But Blackwood, commanding the West Highland's principal station, expected to live apart. He secured the redundant booking office (above) and appealed directly to Conacher for a permanent house:

> Fort William has now been open for [many] months, and still no signs of anything being done. I have taken the liberty of bringing this matter under your personal notice.

The North British directors reluctantly authorised the expenditure of up to £3,600 on company houses. Designed by engineer Carswell, two tenements were erected during 1896, at the angle of Fort William High Street and the new road giving entry, by the gated level crossing, to engine shed and goods yard.[3] At Arnott's suggestion these buildings became 'Tweeddale Place', commemorating the West Highland's opening day. Three brick-built surfacemen's cottages were set by the lineside, opposite the locomotive coaling stage. In addition a small tenement was erected at Crianlarich, where Carswell's men predominated. Cowlairs enginemen held overnight at Fort William obtained a wooden dormitory beside the engine shed, with eight cots and a kitchen; a wash-house (built from spent sleepers and a worn-out boiler) was added later. 'Lodging turns' were a given for drivers and firemen at this date.

Conacher required assurances from every departmental head that adequate rents would be forthcoming, though Arnott warned of Fort William's high burgh rates, while Carswell thought Crianlarich 'outlandish' and recommended concessions. Domestic coal and groceries were expensive everywhere, and surfacemen in particular were difficult to retain. Conacher, however, was inflexible, rejecting a subsequent petition when Tweeddale Place rents were increased. Any reductions would be reflected in West Highland working costs. House rents on the West Highland were not related to North British pay scales, which caused inter-departmental tensions: signalmen, for example, earned 21s per week, while telegraph linesmen had 30s. Deuchars admitted that extra provisions largely absorbed the supplementary payments for boarding relief men, while additional cooking and laundry burdened wives or daughters. (A posting peculiar to the West Highland was the clerk-porter based at Rannoch during the shooting season, to record and despatch game.) Nevertheless, West Highland cottages represented, when put in order, the highest standards of the day: '£500 houses', said Carswell, whose yardstick was £300.

Fort William, Tweeddale Place
William Clarkson, driver
John Russell, driver
Robert Beattie, driver
James McKay, passenger guard
James Blackwood, stationmaster*
James Kay, driver
William Sellars, goods guard

William Gray, clerk (assistant to superintendent Arnott)
Finlay Fraser, telegraph lineman
George Aitchison, telegraph inspector
William Coventry, traffic inspector

*Blackwood, who lived rent-free (like other stationmasters), was persuaded to take one of the larger flats.

Crianlarich
R. Fullarton, signalman
George Bruce, permanent way inspector
Dougal McLaughlin, foreman joiner
John Graham, joiner
John McColl, blacksmith
James McGregor, signal fitter
Alexander Forbes, ballast guard
James Maxwell, foreman platelayer

The stationmasters at Row (Rhu), Shandon, Garelochhead and Arrochar & Tarbet had occupied their cottages late in 1894, though inconvenienced by leaking roofs and other defects. Their colleagues were still homeless:

> Upper Helensburgh, Ardlui, Crianlarich – slated and floors laid, plaster work very damp, caught by frost.
> Tyndrum – partly plastered, caught by frost, floors to lay.
> Bridge of Orchy – slated, plaster work not begun, floors to lay.
> Rannoch – roofed, plaster work not begun.
> Tulloch – slated and plastered, caught by frost.
> Roy Bridge – slated, plaster work caught by frost, floors to lay.
> Spean Bridge – roofed but not slated, plaster work not begun, floors to lay.

In January 1895, Conacher took the work away from Lucas & Aird. Charles Forman, admitting frost damage over Christmas and New Year, complained that the various stationmasters, being on the spot, might have saved the situation 'by lighting fires in all the grates'. He warned that, as with the surfacemen's houses already given over to Carswell's squads, 'your people cannot finish any quicker'.

Lucas & Aird's handover was inevitably untidy. Overtaxed, they had done shoddy work. Carswell, and secretary Wieland too, had underestimated the many tasks to be tackled, and Conacher was insufficiently informed. Of all who suffered in consequence, Rannoch stationmaster William Jamieson fared worst. Promoted from a North British outpost in Northumberland, he found his house not even begun and installed his family in a draughty hut, which Findlay & Co. had occupied during erection of the

Gauer and Rannoch viaducts. They asked £25. To lodge Jamieson elsewhere and pay his expenses while he travelled to duty, which in any case might be impossible, would cost more. Deuchars settled for £20, noting that the hut had 'two good stoves' and might be dismantled later for use elsewhere. The Findlay hut was some distance from the station and too small for Jamieson's furniture, stored nearby but suffering damage, and he could not easily care for his ailing wife, whom he thought to send away. After the heavy snows of January and February 1895 he appealed for a larger shack:

> As there is no appearance of my new house being completed … I would respectfully ask to have the hut lately occupied by [Lucas & Aird's] ganger … transferred from Cruach … if it is now our Company's property.

Six months later, Deuchars minuted:

> [Jamieson] has completely lost heart … and is causing some little trouble … with the rendering of his returns etc. [His] wife caught a chill while living in the wooden house … and died [and] he, having a young family, has had to get a housekeeper. He only got into the new house about the end of June.

At the southern end of the route, Carswell inherited a long list of urgent repairs, but the finished houses were more or less habitable and district superintendent Cunningham maintained pressure for remedial action. In Arnott's fiefdom, north of Ardlui, matters moved slowly, and by October of 1895 Deuchars felt obliged to intervene:

> The Porter and Signalman at Rannoch, the Signalman and his wife and daughter at Spean Bridge, and the Signalman at Tulloch are still living in Waiting Rooms, and the Signalman at Crianlarich in a … hut. [The] men are discontented, having had to live in unsatisfactory houses through one of the most severe winters on record, and … another winter is now facing them …

Conacher abruptly ordered the engineer at once to 'do anything he can to add to the comfort of the men where they are at present situated', pending fresh efforts in 1896. A postal service for the railwaymen of Strathtulla would be one improvement in the longer run. The stationmasters at Ardlui, Bridge of Orchy, Rannoch and Tulloch had been appointed sub-postmasters for the convenience of their districts, and from 1897 a Royal Mail pouch went between Bridge of Orchy and Gortan by the daily goods trains.

Having opted for a more generous provision of company houses, the North British found that the ground already acquired by the West Highland Company at Helensburgh, Rhu Garelochhead and Ardlui gave room enough. It was politic, however, to allow the Colquhouns' factor sight of Carswell's plans. At Shandon and

THE STATION HOTEL,

(At the Terminus of the West Highland Railway),

The Natural Starting Point for INVERNESS and OBAN.

Passengers en route for INVERNESS should break their Journey at FORT WILLIAM—thus avoiding the early start from OBAN—and proceed by Train, via Spean Bridge, over the New Railway Route, thence to Fort Augustus—taking David MacBrayne Ltd. Steamer forward to Inverness, and vice versa.

STATION HOTEL, FORT WILLIAM.

THIS Magnificent and Sumptuously Furnished HOTEL (built in 1896), is erected on an elevated and commanding site, overlooking an extensive panorama of the grandest Loch and Mountain Scenery in the Highlands—LOCH LINNHE, LOCH EIL, THE GREAT GLEN OF CALEDONIA, and BEN NEVIS.

Over 100 Apartments; every Room commanding a Magnificent View absolutely unsurpassed in the Highlands.

PLEASURE GROUNDS EXTENDING OVER THREE ACRES.
TERRACED WALKS, TENNIS COURTS, GOLF COURSE, BOATING, FISHING.

Electric Lighting Throughout.   Sanitary arrangements on most Modern Principles.

Parties wishing to ascend BEN NEVIS should stay at the STATION HOTEL, it being the nearest and most convenient First-Class Hotel.

POSTING.   MODERATE CHARGES.

The Hotel Porters and Omnibuses attend the arrival of all trains.

(In connection with the STATION HOTEL, BRORA, SUTHERLAND).

GEORGE SINCLAIR, Proprietor.

Arrochar & Tarbet, additional parcels of land were purchased from the Luss Trustees. Garelochhead's resident railwaymen included a permanent way inspector and a lineman, whose claim was urged by telegraph superintendent Archibald Clement:

> [Ramsay] is ... far away from the station, and ... he should be within easy call seeing that the line is single and worked by tablet, and that any interruption causes so much delay ...

All these dwellings were completed during 1896, together with cottages for the signalmen north from Crianlarich.[4]

On Arnott's urgent plea, improvements were authorised at Fort William yard. Looping up two sidings made for easier marshalling. During 1895 additional sidings were inserted in the 'V' of Banavie Junction. A town-side loop was put in where the opening-day platform had stood, opposite the belatedly completed goods shed; it trailed in at the gated level crossing – the points protected, like the crossing, by the outer home signal. (Shunting required possession of the seawall 'main'.) A side-on loading bank was added, directly accessible from the town and with ample livestock pens. If a derailment isolated the station, or the rare extremes of wind, rain and tide flooded the pierhead, the bank could be turned to passenger use.[5]

In anticipation of the expansion to be stimulated by the new railway, Fort William had undertaken an ambitious water supply scheme, tapping the River Nevis. A new abbatoir complemented Angus Cameron's auction mart (see Chapter 5). With new roads laid out on the rising ground behind the town (their pattern is still identifiable), both Cameron of Lochiel and Mrs Cameron-Campbell gave off feus. On a prime site overlooking pier and pierhead, the large new 'Station Hotel' was soon under construction. Arnott, concerned for his company's dignity (and his own), was dismayed to discover that the North British had no say in the name chosen.[6] Building materials were being delivered by sea to the former distillery pier, where West Highland rights proved flimsy – another chink in Arnott's authority. Distiller MacDonald's original Board of Trade disposition forbad charges, and he had relied on private arrangements with those who used his quay. The North British needed formal powers, for which the West Highland Acts made no provision. It was doubtfully worthwhile to install a crane. For railway traffic at the pier and goods handled by Camerons, the North British carters, Conacher instructed Arnott that he might apply wagon-load rates; he should avoid confrontation with other shippers but encourage them to 'volunteer' payment. Sea-borne coal continued to be landed, in competition with the West Highland.

Opposite: Advertisement, Station Hotel (later Highland Hotel), Fort William, 1907. (Courtesy of the Scottish Railway Preservation Society)

Chapter 14

'Inverlair & Kingussie', Banavie, Ballachulish and Ben Nevis

Laggan

During 1893 Charles Forman, casting around for his next venture, conducted surveys on his own account not only in the Great Glen, but along Loch Laggan. He planned to link West Highland Inverlair (Tulloch) with the Highland Railway in Strathspey. A Laggan and Spean feeder line from Lochaber had been suggested as early as the 1840s, when the rail route from Perth to Inverness by Tay and Spey was first surveyed; the proposed Fort William Railway of 1863 would have taken the same course, from a junction (at Etteridge or Newtonmore) with the Highland Company's newly completed Perth–Inverness main line.[1] To preserve the Great Glen treaty, Andrew Dougall and John Conacher were reluctantly ready to endorse a Laggan scheme, which would not menace the Highland's Inverness redoubt. The possibility had been recognised in the 1889 Agreement, and it was still, in Dougall's estimation, the lesser evil (see Appendix). He met with Cameron of Lochiel; unspecified West Highland 'representatives' examined Forman's layout; and a West Highland Inverlair & Kingussie Extension Bill was announced for parliamentary session 1893/4.[2] That the Highland and North British boards were fully in favour is doubtful. They were not called upon to decide, because Forman's Great Glen project languished. An alternative was now unnecessary and no Laggan bill was lodged, but the episode contributed to the Highland Company's suspicions of North British duplicity, which broke out a year later (see Chapter 10).

After the collapse and repair of the Great Glen Agreement in 1894/5, Forman kept his two schemes in play. Besides holding out the prizes that might accrue if the Ten Years Truce could be nullified yet again, thus forcing Highland and North British into another battle for Inverness, he also pushed the advantages of a Laggan link. The Aberdeen-based Great North of Scotland Company responded: they contemplated a route to Fort William, and eventually Mallaig, via Boat of Garten and Kingussie. On Conacher's instructions, William Arnott monitored Forman's activities, ordering his own subordinates to be vigilant. Stationmaster Dorward at Tulloch noted the engineer's arrival by the Kingussie coach, with maps and plans – and his luggage labels indicated a journey from Aberdeen. Arnott himself showed a talent for espionage. Informed of strangers at the Lochiel Arms Hotel (Banavie), he found a pretext to call, furtively checking the register. The visitors were indeed a Great North of Scotland party who looked over the Mallaig route, where construction would not begin for eighteen months more. But the Aberdeen company's interest soon shifted to the Invergarry & Fort Augustus Railway and its possible extension to Inverness, where they might join hands with the invader. Elgin–Inverness running powers had always eluded the Great North and here was one more opportunity to obtain them.3

Banavie Branch

During 1893/5, completion of the West Highland Banavie branch remained with Lucas & Aird, who were also still at work on Fort William station and Nevis distillery sidings. In July 1894 the embankments were half-formed and the girders of the Lochy viaduct not yet secured. The contractor's base was moved to Banavie, but their pugs (two were retained) ran to and from Fort William yard, besides hauling fill and ballast from Auchindaul on tracks now carrying passenger traffic. North British irritation at the barely finished state of the entire West Highland route was reflected in what seem petty questions. Should a charge be made when Lucas & Aird were supplied with a brake van and guard? Should a pug driver, though in possession of a Caledonian Company certificate, be sent to Cowlairs for examination by locomotive superintendent Holmes? (He was.)

Carswell, the North British engineer, insisted that catch points be installed at Banavie Junction. Though the branch would be worked, 'one engine in steam', by

Lochy viaduct, West Highland Railway, Banavie branch. The castellated piers match nearby Inverlochy Castle. (J. Alsop collection)

Opening of Banavie Branch for General Traffic.

The Banavie Branch, which extends from Banavie Junction, West Highland Railway, to the West Highland Railway Wharf on the Caledonian Canal near Banavie Station will be opened for Traffic purposes on

FRIDAY, 31st MAY 1895.

The Branch will be worked by Train Staff only, and in strict accordance with Rules 355–374 inclusive, with this important distinction that no Train Staff Tickets will be used.

NOTE.—There are no fixed Signals on the Banavie Branch, but in lieu thereof the Train Staff for the Branch has attached to it the Key for the Points giving access to Messrs Lucas & Aird's Siding (which connects with the Banavie Branch between Banavie Junction and Banavie Station) and to the Sidings at Banavie Station. It necessarily follows that these Sidings can only be worked by a Train the Driver of which is in possession of the Train Staff.

Inspector Hogg will attend and see the foregoing brought into force.

J. CONACHER,
General Manager.

EDINBURGH, 29*th May* 1895.

Acknowledgment to be signed, cut off, and returned to Office of Superintendent of the Line,
Edinburgh, by first train.

Date,_____1895.

I hereby acknowledge to have received ___ copies of Circular (**M—No. 2809**), dated 29th May 1895, in reference to "Opening of Banavie Branch for General Traffic," to which I shall attend.

Signature,_____

Occupation,_____

(4–C)   Station,_____

staff-and-key, Forman urged the prudential addition of interlocking and signals at the Banavie terminus. When Conacher first appraised the West Highland in 1892, his inclination had been to abandon the branch, substituting a Banavie station for rail-steamer exchange at the Caledonian Canal crossing on the hoped-for Mallaig Extension.[4] Work ceased; but he subsequently accepted that, for the short term at least, the line must be made and a house provided for the Banavie stationmaster. (Arnott was anxious for the sensibilities of First Class tourists, going between train and steamer, who might dislike passing a railwayman's door, and recommended that the cottage be set back from the footpath.) The Junction signalman obtained one of Carswell's temporary wooden dwellings (see Chapter 7). Major Marindin, who inspected the line in May of 1895, was displeased 'to find on a new branch ... rails which had previously been used', but did not insist on relaying. Lucas & Aird had put down worn rails from their main contract.[5] Public traffic began on 1 June.

The Banavie branch was a substitute for the Caledonian Canal link (Spean Bridge–Loch Lochy) dropped from the West Highland Bill of 1888/9 (see Appendix). MacBrayne's summer vessels did not make the passage of Banavie locks, (dramatic 'Neptune's

FORT WILLIAM AND ARISAIG

THE Royal Mail Coach leaves Fort William Daily at 12.30 P.M., arriving at Arisaig at 7.30 P.M.; leaving Arisaig at 8.15 A.M., arriving at Fort William at 3.15 P.M., in time to catch the Steamer for Oban and Train for South (West Highland Railway).

FARES TO ARISAIG, 11s.

For further information apply at the Post Office, Fort William.

M'GREGOR & CAMERON, Proprietors.

N.B.—M'G. & C. are now carrying on the Coaching and Posting Business at the Stables, Gordon Square, Fort William; Alexandra Hotel Stables, Fort William; and Lochiel Arms Hotel Stables, Banavie.

For further information apply as above, or at the Office, 43 High St., Fort William.

Above: Notice, Arisaig mail cart, 1897. (Author's collection)
Opposite: North British Railway traffic notice, opening of West Highland Railway Banavie branch, 1895. (Author's collection)

Banavie (now Banavie Pier) station, *c.* 1930 – renamed in 1901 when another 'Banavie' opened on the West Highland Mallaig Extension. (W. Rear collection/Courtesy of the Northern British Railway Study Group)

Staircase'), but turned at the upper basin, whence a 'horse omnibus' connected with Corpach, where the Oban steamers terminated. Now tourists and other travellers would transfer by the branch trains, leaving or joining the Oban boats at Fort William. That they were likely to break their journey in the town gratified hoteliers and shopkeepers. Designated a goods and passenger railhead for all the country west to Arisaig and Moidart, Banavie afforded some compensation for the lost line to Roshven, until its Mallaig successor could be approved and built. Conacher first intended only passenger provision in conjunction with the steamers, but sidings and a crane were provided. Goods traffic included distillery grain brought down the canal from MacDonald's suppliers around the Moray Firth. The summer timetable was initially generous; in 1896, it detailed eight passenger trains in both directions (including through Glasgow workings which reversed in Fort William), plus a daily goods train which returned 'mixed' to Fort William. Diminutive 4-4-0 tank engines were usually employed.

Ballachulish Extension

Caledonian and North British had agreed in principle to share the district between Oban and Fort William (see Chapter 10). Though bad-tempered exchanges continued, proposals for a Callander & Oban branch to Ballachulish Ferry and a West Highland branch (styled 'Extension') to Onich and North Ballachulish were submitted to Parliament in 1895/6.[6] The 1895 General Election interrupted negotiations, several directors on both sides being MPs (including Caledonian chairman Joseph Bolton). The two Ballachulish bills were framed on the basis that a through-rail connection was for the present superfluous (cf. Highland and North British claims that any Great Glen scheme was premature). One line would serve Benderloch, Appin and Ballachulish, feeding traffic to the Callander & Oban at Connel Ferry; the other (literally an extension in that it continued the line that crossed Fort William pierhead) would tie Nether Lochaber to the West Highland and tap Ardgour and Morvern at Corran Ferry. A swing bridge over Loch Leven at Ballachulish Narrows was to carry a tramway, connecting both branches with Ballachulish slate quarries while allowing room for a public road.

The Caledonian claimed to prefer a high-level bridge, facilitating a conventional rail link at some future date without awkward gradients on either shore. Meanwhile, shipping would be entirely unimpeded. To make doubly sure that Caledonian pretensions were contained, the North British urged a wider neutral zone: the Callander & Oban branch should terminate at Kentallen, with the shared tramway extended south to develop the granite workings there. In the event, Parliament approved both promotions as first lodged – save that the swing bridge, and thus the common tramway, was disallowed. In 1896/7, the Callander & Oban Company would obtain powers to continue their line from Ballachulish Ferry to Ballachulish village and quarries. The Fort William–North Ballachulish line would never be built.

Arnott, very willing to expand his territory, had reported in favour of an exclusively West Highland branch, crossing the Narrows and reaching to the village. Much Ballachulish slate, sent by sea to the Clyde or via the Caledonian Canal to the east coast, was consigned forward to inland destinations. This traffic would be captured once direct rail transit had eliminated transhipment. Ballachulish and district were little inferior to Fort William in population; their coals and general merchandise, carried by coasting vessels, might be won for the West Highland. Arnott also cited 'the great tourist traffic to Glen Coe', certain to increase when a nearer railhead was created, and he anticipated that MacBrayne's steamers would give new train connections at Ballachulish. Nigel MacKenzie, who once again interviewed prospective parliamentary witnesses, looked to the livestock traffic of the Ardgour hinterland. Sheep and cattle were still walked to Corran Ferry, some continuing to Fort William, some going by Ballachulish Ferry to Callander & Oban Tyndrum, now rivalled by West Highland Bridge of Orchy. Rail shipment from Corran would be popular, shortening these droves.

Conacher was sceptical. He set little store by residential development at Onich or along Loch Linnhe south from Fort William.[7] He aimed above all to exclude the Caledonian from Lochaber, and from any say in the West Highland Mallaig Extension, and his own calculations warned that traffic over a through line would tend to the Callander & Oban. Were the North Ballachulish branch built, Conacher intended a limited and purely local passenger service, utilising the locomotives and rolling stock lying over at Fort William between Glasgow workings. As a safeguard against Caledonian machinations, the powers granted in 1896 were sufficient, without undertaking construction. (The North British would make sure, on to 1914, that these West Highland powers were twice renewed.) Disappointed communities and accusations of betrayal could be ignored – unless the Caledonian were tempted to make another probe beyond the Loch Leven frontier.

The Callander & Oban Ballachulish branch, opened in 1903, would survive until 1966 (cf. the Invergarry & Fort Augustus Railway, which lost its passenger service in 1933 and closed completely after the Second World War). An integrated railway system for the western Highlands remained Charles Forman's vision (albeit a vision mixed with self-interest), but direct rail connection between Oban and Inverness, by Ballachulish, Fort William and the Great Glen, was from the mid-1890s a receding prospect. And completion of the Highland Company's Aviemore cut-off in 1898, shortening the Perth–Inverness trunk route, told decisively against a West Highland-cum-Great Glen alternative. Scheduled to the West Highland Ballachulish Extension Act – thus not entirely a dead letter – were the terms that finally resolved the Fort William foreshore dispute. To preserve access to Loch Linnhe, the North Ballachulish line must exit the town by a low viaduct, not an impassable embankment, while accommodation bridges or subways must be given to loch-side villa owners. Severed burgh land was to be made into an 'ornamental garden'. With the line unbuilt, these provisions would become academic. Meanwhile, the North British had resisted Major Marindin's full recommendations, and the Board of Trade, diluting their award, permitted sleepered crossings instead of footbridges at station and signal box (see Chapter 4). A watchman – he endured the West Highland's first winter without shelter – had already been appointed at the gated level crossing.[8]

Ben Nevis

A mountain railway for Ben Nevis must enhance West Highland summer traffic. If the idea did not originate with Charles Forman, he was certainly ready to entertain it. In 1888/9 the project had been discussed (though not the means of operation) and was known to the West Highland promoters. A meteorological observatory had been established at the summit in 1883, served by a well-made pony track from Glen Nevis. This encouraged tourist ascents, but the line to which distiller MacDonald alluded in his parliamentary evidence would have followed the traditional route from Lochy Bridge, under the Ben's northern cliffs. Of several unsuccessful attempts to advance the scheme, only one took firm shape; it would have run 6 miles from Nevis Bridge through the Nevis Gorge then climbed abruptly to the summit plateau.

Opposite: Advertisement, Spean Bridge Hotel, 1907. All tourist literature featured Ben Nevis. (Courtesy of the Scottish Railway Preservation Society)

Postscript

Construction of the Mallaig Extension began in 1897; it opened in 1901. No 'north of Strome' line would be achieved; but the Highland Company's Dingwall & Skye route was continued (1897) from Strome Ferry to Kyle of Lochalsh, the terminus first intended. For this purpose a parliamentary grant balanced the state assistance which the West Highland Company had received.

The Mallaig line's Treasury Guarantee ran until 1931, but would be rendered almost valueless by the terms of Decontrol (1919) when the railways returned to

Remains of Invergarry & Fort Augustus Railway: trackbed and pier, Loch Ness. (J. L. Stevenson Collection)

private operation after the First World War. Rating relief was confirmed by an action of declarator in the Scottish courts. (General de-rating of the railway industry came in the 1930s.)

1896/7 saw a triangular contest, when Highland, Invergarry & Fort Augustus and North British-West Highland competed to occupy the 30 miles between Fort Augustus and Inverness. All three bills failed. The Invergarry & Fort Augustus Company chose to build (1897–1901) their authorised line, which exhausted their resources. From 1903 it was worked by the Highland Railway, though unconnected with the Highland system. From 1907 the North British took over and in 1914 they finally purchased the bankrupt Invergarry & Fort Augustus, now fated to a brief existence as a hopelessly unprofitable West Highland branch.

William Arnott would have only one successor. George Innes, as district superintendent at Fort William, added the Mallaig line to his command. In 1908 the West Highland was absorbed at last into the North British, to be managed entirely from Glasgow. By 1905 the West Highland's overall line speed could be set at 40 mph, but with numerous restrictions. Between 1906 and 1914 a new generation of North British 4-4-0s and 0-6-0s came into service. All this fixed the character of the route, though with successive changes in locomotive types and traffic, until the end of steam in the 1960s. Two trains in each direction between Glasgow and Mallaig,

Remains of Invergarry & Fort Augustus Railway: abutment of High Bridge viaduct, Glen Spean. (Courtesy of I. Henshaw)

supplemented by Extension locals, became the standard provision, expanding each summer season. The Banavie branch kept a vestigial passenger service, connecting with the summer steamers on the Caledonian Canal, until 1939. The Arrochar & Tarbet locals endured to 1964.

Above: Banavie (Pier) station building, *c.* 1955 – since refurbished as a private dwelling. (Courtesy of W. Gee)
Below: Gortan (Gorton) in 2015 – a minimal facility for engineering and maintenance. (Courtesy of Norman MacNab)

Appendix

The West Highland Company's substantive powers were:

Bill, 1888/9 (Act of 1889)	
No. 1 Craigendoran–Crianlarich	authorised
No. 2 Craigendoran–Fort William	authorised
No. 4 Crianlarich spur to Callander & Oban Railway	authorised
No. 6 Fort William, old fort to pierhead	authorised
Bill, 1889-90 (Act of 1890)	
No. 2 (Deviation) Glen Spean	authorised
No. 3 (Deviation) Torlundy–Fort William	authorised
No. 4 Extension of No. 6 (1889) across Fort William pierhead	authorised
Nos 5–7 Banavie branch, with back shunt to pier	authorised
1888/9 No. 3 Fort William–Roshven	*struck out*
1888/9 No. 5 Spean Bridge–Loch Lochy	*deleted by promoters*
1889/90 No. 1 (Deviation) Cruach–Corrour	*struck out*

Draft Great Glen Agreement, Westminster, 3 July 1889

1. The Highland Company no longer to oppose the West Highland Bill.
2. The North British Company and the West Highland promoters undertake 'not to promote directly or indirectly, nor to support the promotion by any other company or persons, nor to contribute to nor work any railway north or east of Banavie for ten years after the opening of the West Highland Railway to Fort William'.
3. The Highland Company and the North British Company to revise (but preserve) terms of exchange at Perth.
4. £500 to be paid by the North British Company 'towards the Highland Company's costs of opposing the West Highland Bill'.

An addendum allowed the possibility of a Glen Spean–Strathspey link 'between the West Highland line at or near Inverlair and the Highland Railway at any point between Kingussie and Dalwhinnie'.

Notes

Chapter 1

1. The adjusted steamer timetables injured Fort William as a market town: 'Our customers are carried to Oban.'
2. The Stirling & Western Direct, engineered by Formans & McCall, had offered the North British independent entry to Stirling, bypassing Caledonian Larbert.
3. If the balance of West Highland income, after deduction of 50 per cent for working expenses, did not generate a 4½ per cent return, the North British would find the difference, remitting part of their earnings on through traffic.
4. The West Highland Bill went first to the House of Lords.

Chapter 2

1. From Craigendoran to Loch Lomond, rock and soil intermingled – it was cheaper, and quicker, to deal with one or the other.
2. For installing this basic telephone system, the North British telegraph superintendent was granted a bonus.
3. It is uncertain when the viaducts on these sections were approved. Marindin's May expedition had ended at Gortan.
4. Dr Cameron-Miller, surgeon at Belford Hospital, became 'medical officer to the West Highland Railway'. He published an account of his experiences, on which these paragraphs are based.
5. The tree survived all subsequent alterations, until in the 1970s the railway layout was entirely swept away.

Chapter 3

1. The Crianlarich spur and the Banavie branch were not ready.

2. The West Highland seal conjoined the insignia of Dunbartonshire, Perthshire, Argyll and Inverness-shire, the four counties through which the line passed.
3. From 1892 the North British dominated the West Highland board.
4. Lochiel, Conservative MP for Inverness-shire from the 1860s, had foreseen that the electoral reforms of 1884/5 would transform political fortunes in Highland constituencies. Proactive measures might placate the new voters, and he had urged the Napier Commission in this direction.
5. Fort William was a police burgh from 1873, hence 'police commissioners'.

Chapter 4

1. A *through* station, cf. the West Highland *terminal* station as later built.
2. The then shingle beach is buried beneath the road layout and carpark created in the 1970s.
3. The harbour, obliterated in the 1970s, was a natural one, located behind a gravel spit deposited by a hillside burn.
4. Marindin also re-examined the 9 miles from Spean Bridge, cursorily treated at the end of his long Monday, which had begun at Tyndrum.

Chapter 5

1. Carting was difficult – one reason why distiller MacDonald built his own pier.
2. In later years Glasgow–Mallaig and Mallaig–Glasgow trains, reversing at Fort William, were 'topped and tailed' as required by relieving engine or duty pilot. With all-corridor, gangwayed stock, these manoeuvres became safer (though no less time-consuming) and the short platforms tolerable. Arrivals routinely overshot on the sea-side road to free the throat points. The between-the-piers tracks became two sidings, where coaches could be stabled, and the cross-over inside the station was seldom used.
3. The 4th Baron Abinger avoided involvement with the West Highland Company, though his father had been a key promoter and first chairman.
4. The sidings at Spean Bridge were relatively lavish, in anticipation of a larger Great Glen drove traffic than would ever materialise.

Chapter 6

1. Summer cooperation in some degree contradicted their intense, wasteful Clyde coast competition, which was eventually reduced from the 1890s by pooling agreements. All three companies had steamer subsidiaries.

2. The Helensburgh terminus would become 'Helensburgh Central', as against West Highland 'Upper Helensburgh'.
3. The through vehicles to and from London Kings Cross would evolve into the West Highland 'sleeper', which today runs from London Euston.
4. The Callander & Oban Bill included harbour improvements at Oban and extension of their Ballachulish branch to Ballachulish village, see also Chapter 14.
5. Under the legislation of 1896, only Board of Trade approval was needed, given an acceptable layout and adequate input from proprietors and local authorities. Set-piece parliamentary confrontation was avoided.
6. In later years, exuberant Fort William enginemen liked to demonstrate that, with water taken at Ardlui, a reliable locomotive could complete the journey without further replenishment.
7. They would remain so into the 1960s, more than a dozen years after railway nationalisation. The spur saw occasional extraordinary use, excursions and, introduced between the First and Second World Wars, a return summer working between Glasgow and Oban, via Craigendoran.

Chapter 7

1. Forman had conceived the West Highland (like his Clyde, Ardrishaig & Crinan), in almost light railway terms. North British requirements and post-1894 improvement produced the line we now know.
2. Monzie Villa: the site is now occupied by St Mary's Roman Catholic church.

Chapter 8

1. Glasgow Eastfield engine shed dates from 1904. In the 1890s Cowlairs was general depot, shed and locomotive works.
2. Implying a return to Bridge of Orchy.
3. Carswell was commended by the North British board.

Chapter 9

1. It was the West Highland's only tunnel, until the Treig deviation of the 1930s. (But Forman planned two bores west of Glenfinnan, at the summit of his Roshven line.) Sir James wanted a conservative masonry viaduct. Forman's signature girder spans otherwise prevail all along the route.
2. Lochiel owned a detached property on Rannoch Moor.
3. The West Highland as first authorised would have crossed the River Spean at

Inverlair Falls, crossing back above Monessie Gorge.
4. The Fort William–Tyndrum line proposed in 1874 would have been less difficult, in that narrow gauge permitted tighter curves and stiffer gradients. Engineer Walrond-Smith intended to terrace the Glasgow & North Western below Glen Coe's Aonach Eagach ridge, through short tunnels and avalanche shelters.
5. There is no suggestion that the Duke wanted a Rosneath branch, see Chapter 6.
6. A Burton-on-Trent newspaper carried the story.
7. Colonel Walker's old lodge was situated on higher ground east of Cruach, on the ancient bridle path from Rannoch into Lochaber.
8. Glen Douglas would flit in and out of the passenger timetables (Arrochar & Tarbet shuttle). Gortan remained mysterious – from time to time discovered by journalists in search of copy.

Chapter 10

1. The Lanarkshire & Dumbartonshire Railway, extending the Glasgow Central, would bring the Caledonian to Dumbarton, forcing the North British to concede joint ownership of their Vale of Leven line and Loch Lomond steamers.
2. Cf. Walrond-Smith's first intentions in 1882/3 (see Chapter 4). Presumably, had both their lines been approved, Callander & Oban and Highland would have shared a station at Fort William, eliminating the improbable tunnel.
3. The reference is to MacDonald's celebrated Long John whisky.
4. These months included the West Highland's first, unexpectedly severe, winter (see Chapter 8).

Chapter 11

1. Unenthusiastic about any scheme 'north of Strome', the Highland hoped, by accepting one in principle, to see off the West Highland Extension. They lent the Garve & Ullapool promoters their engineer. Chamberlain, though a witness for the West Highland in 1889, also had the Ullapool scheme in mind.
2. To reduce rock work west from Kinlochailort (Simpson needed eight tunnels), Forman suggested rack-and-pinion. He favoured a commodious harbour inside Loch Nevis, better sheltered than Mallaig bay.
3. Simpson became a North British director.
4. Baillie *retained* the seat, having won the by-election following Crofter-Liberal McGregor's sudden retirement earlier in 1895.
5. That Dalziel might become the Treasury's representative when the Liberals regained office was a North British nightmare.

Chapter 12

1. Anderson & Shaw of Inverness, not Innes & MacKay, had handled Forman's previous project.
2. Forman conflated the Highland Company's proposed line via Gairlochy and his own earlier surveys, abandoning his direct Roy Bridge–Invergloy entry to the Great Glen.
3. Keyden, Strange and Girvan were old associates of James Forman, father of Charles. David Reid, becoming senior partner, eventually guided the Invergarry & Fort Augustus.
4. Matheson and Cunninghame had Caledonian Railway associations, which jangled North British nerves.
5. Forman suggested that the Invergarry & Fort Augustus acquire the Caledonian Canal – and with it the annual subsidy dispensed by the Canal Commissioners. This idea, it seems, was not pursued.

Chapter 13

1. Save for the derailment near Upper Helensburgh in August 1894, see Chapter 7.
2. Though double-headed, the train was lightly loaded. The second engine had made an unbalanced journey north.
3. The tenements concealed the little harbour behind the seawall, see Chapter 4.
4. It bears saying that North British railwaymen, to better themselves or escape from city conditions, competed for West Highland appointments. Character references survive from clergymen, departmental heads and others who might carry weight.
5. Much detail of the original layout at Fort William between pierhead and old fort, lost to the modern A82 bypass, is preserved in the large-scale 1901 series OS map.
6. It later became the Highland Hotel, but the older Chevalier, on the corner of the High Street and the pierhead (and today converted to shops), was renamed the Station Hotel.

Chapter 14

1. Strictly speaking the Highland Company, subsuming the Inverness & Perth Junction, came into being only in 1865. Cameron of Lochiel, Lord Abinger and distiller Donald MacDonald, protagonists of the West Highland Railway twenty-five years later, all supported the Fort William Railway.
2. Junction with the Highland Railway would have been (presumably) at Newtonmore.
3. The Great North made two exploratory expeditions to Lochaber. Space does not

permit discussion of that company's many attempts to outflank the Highland Railway. The Great North–Highland conflict, like other deep-seated inter-company rivalries, would fade away before 1914.

4. The Extension station was eventually sited immediately east of the Caledonian Canal. A different plan shows station and siding on the west bank, aligned with the Tomonie curve.

5. Noting the improved condition of the route north from Craigendoran, Marindin permitted a small increase in average line speed.

6. Also before Parliament in 1895/6 were the Mallaig Guarantee Bill, the Invergarry & Fort Augustus Bill and the Light Railways Bill.

7. MacKenzie kept summer quarters at Onich, commuting to Fort William by MacBrayne's steamers.

8. From the 1920s the gates would be remotely controlled from the signal box.

Select Bibliography

Dow, George, *The Story of the West Highland* (LNER, 1944).
McGregor, John, *100 Years of the West Highland Railway* (ScotRail, 1994).
McGregor, John, *The West Highland Railway: Plans, Politics and People** (Birlinn/ John Donald, 2005).
Ross, David, *The North British Railway* (Stenlake, 2014).
Thomas, John, *The West Highland Railway* (David & Charles, 1965).

*Based, like *The New Railway*, on primary sources – from National Records of Scotland, Edinburgh; PRO, Kew and West Highland Museum/Lochaber Archive. Fort William.

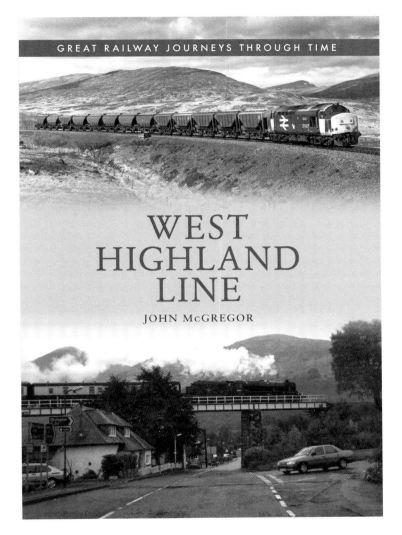

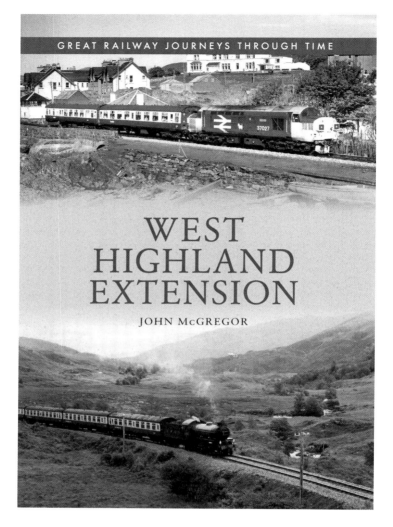

West Highland Extension: Great Railway Journeys Through Time

John McGregor

In this book, a companion to his volume on the West Highland Line, Dr John McGregor uses a wide selection of period and modern photographs to bring the history and dramatic landscape of the Mallaig Extension to life.

978 1 4456 1338 3
96 pages, full colour and illustrated throughout

Available from all good bookshops or to order direct
from our website www.amberley-books.com

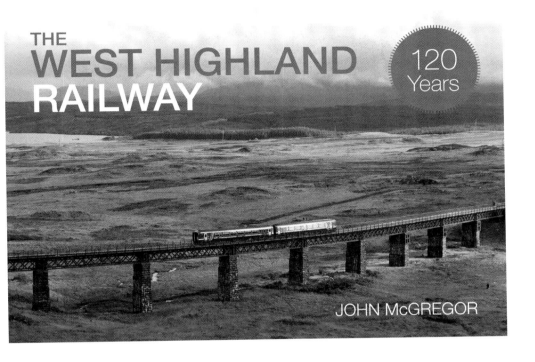

The West Highland Railway: 120 Years

John McGregor

In this profusely illustrated book, Dr John McGregor takes a look at this famous line, from its construction to the present day.

978 1 4456 3345 9
128 pages, full colour and illustrated throughout

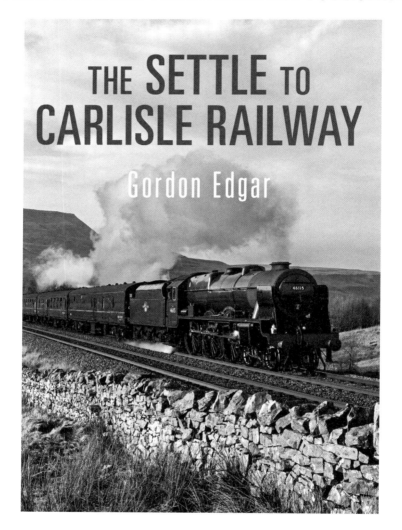

The Settle to Carlisle Railway

Gordon Edgar

With a collection of striking photographs, Gordon Edgar tells the story of arguably one of the most dramatic lines in northern England – the Settle–Carlisle Railway.

978 1 4456 3961 1
96 pages, full colour and illustrated throughout